THE CATHOLIC UNIVERSITY OF AMERICA
STUDIES IN AMERICAN CHURCH HISTORY

VOL. 5

FRANCISCAN MISSIONS IN TEXAS

(1690-1793)

AMS PRESS
NEW YORK

THE CATHOLIC UNIVERSITY OF AMERICA
STUDIES IN AMERICAN CHURCH HISTORY

VOL. V

THE FRANCISCAN MISSIONS IN TEXAS
(1690-1793)

BY
THOMAS P. O'ROURKE, C.S.B., A.M.

A DISSERTATION

SUBMITTED TO THE FACULTY OF PHILOSOPHY OF THE CATHOLIC
UNIVERSITY OF AMERICA IN PARTIAL FULFILLMENT OF
THE REQUIREMENTS FOR THE DEGREE OF
DOCTOR OF PHILOSOPHY

WASHINGTON, D. C.
1927

247.9764
Or6F

Library of Congress Cataloging in Publication Data

O'Rourke, Thomas Patrick, 1889-
  The Franciscan missions in Texas (1690-1793)

  Reprint of the author's thesis, Catholic University
of America, 1927, which was issued as v. 5 of the
Catholic University of America. Studies in American
church history.
  Bibliography: p.
  1. Franciscans—Missions. 2. Missions—Texas.
I. Title. II. Series: Catholic University of
America. Studies in American church history, v. 5.
BV2803.T4076 1974   271'.3'0764   73-3559
ISBN 0-404-57755-5

Nihil Obstat: VERY REV. F. FORSTER, C.S.B.
Nihil Obstat: †RT. REV. THOMAS J. SHAHAN, D.D.
Imprimatur: †MOST REV. MICHAEL J. CURLEY, D.D.
May 14, 1927.

Reprinted from the edition of 1927, Washington D.C.
First AMS edition published, 1974
Manufactured in the United States of America

International Standard Book Number
Complete Set: 0-404-57750-4
Volume 5: 0-404-57755-5

AMS PRESS, INC.
New York, N.Y. 10003

PREFACE

The object of this essay is to bring together for the first time from the sources and printed historical works the history of the Franciscan Missions in Texas from 1690 to 1793. Within the past decade the scholarship and the enthusiasm of Dr. Herbert Eugene Bolton of the University of California have created a larger interest in Texas missionary history. Through his own publications, as well as through those of his students, a considerable number of manuscripts have been studied and published on this question. Although none of these works has dealt exclusively with the story of Franciscan efforts in our Hispanic Southwest, they all contain materials that may be woven into a logical and complete narrative.

This we have attempted to do in the following pages. The scattered condition of the civil archives of Texas; their uncatalogued state at the present time; and the grave difficulty we have encountered in having documents copied in the Mexican archives, owing to the unsettled political conditions in that country during the past two years, have to a certain extent confined our researches to the published works and collections of sources in the manuscript material in the Library of Congress. Chief among the collections of documents we have consulted are the Bolton Transcripts and the Dunn Transcripts. For the former collection there is a serviceable (manuscript) catalogue. The Dunn Transcripts number over seventeen thousand pages. Neither collection of documents, however, is exclusively Texan; and while their yield is comparatively small for the history of the Franciscans in that State, they contain collateral documents which have thrown much light on our study.

It is a story filled with splendid deeds that is outlined in this essay—one that, when all the documentary evidence is brought to light, will take its place alongside the striking series of victories for the Christian Faith so eloquently told by Father Zephyrin Engelhardt, O. F. M., in his *Missions and Missionaries in California* and his *Franciscans in Arizona*.

The long series of unsuccessful explorations and expeditions, northward and eastward from Mexico City, into the present State of Texas would seem at first sight to lead to the conclusion that the Spanish colonial government was not cognizant of the vast territories that lay beyond the Rio Grande del Norte. And as the story develops, it would look as if the one thing needed to arouse the spirit of colonization in Texas was the steady advance of the French after La Salle's tragic venture in Texas in 1685-1687. But it is the opinion of historians that even had the French intrusion not occurred and even had French and Spanish rivalry for the conquest of the Gulf Coast not arisen, the Franciscans and the civil authorities would eventually have carried out a systematic exploration and evangelization of the lands beyond the Great River of the North. The extended *Historia de la Iglesia en Mexico,* which is now in course of publication by Father Mariano Cuevas, S.J., of Mexico City, has not touched the subjects which could be of value for our work; although the four volumes he has so far published have greatly aided us in realizing the historical background of our study.

An essay of this nature can do no more than put the entire chain of historical facts in strict chronological order. This we have done; in the expectation that, as conditions in Mexico become more nearly normal, we shall be able to add to the narrative as given here many unpublished sources which describe the noble courage and self-sacrifice of the followers of St. Francis in America's Lone Star State.

A work of this kind can hardly be done unaided. We owe therefore, an expression of gratitude to many who have assisted us. To the Superior-General of the Congregation of St. Basil, the Very Rev. F. Forster, C.S.B., Toronto, Canada, we offer our thanks for the leave of absence which made our graduate studies possible. To the Faculty of the School of Philosophy of the Catholic University of America the writer extends his appreciation of the many kindnesses that have been shown to him; and in particular to the Rev. Dr. Guilday, Professor of Church History, who has guided this study.

THOMAS PATRICK O'ROURKE.

CONTENTS

	PAGE
PREFACE	iii

CHAPTER

I.	THE COMING OF THE FRANCISCANS TO NEW SPAIN (1522–1675)	1
II.	THE APPROACH OF THE MISSIONARIES TO TEXAS (1675–1689)	8
III.	THE QUERÉTARAN MISSIONS—I: (1690–1731)	18
IV.	THE QUERÉTARAN MISSIONS—II: (1731–1763)	36
V.	THE ZACATECAN MISSIONS (1716–1793)	44
VI.	THE QUERÉTARAN—SAN FERNANDIAN MISSIONS(1757–1769)	64
VII.	THE ADMINISTRATION OF THE MISSIONS	74
VIII.	SOURCES FOR EARLY TEXAS CATHOLIC HISTORY	94
INDEX		102

CHAPTER I.

THE COMING OF THE FRANCISCANS TO NEW SPAIN (1522-1675).

Few aspects of missionary history present more attractive pages to the general reader and the student than the work done during the past seven centuries by the Franciscans. This was evidenced by the world-wide interest shown during the past year (1926) by Catholic and non-Catholic writers in lauding the Poor Little Man of Assisi and his humble followers in making that year a veritable Franciscan jubilee.

During a large part of the seven hundred years of Franciscan activity, the Friars have woven into the fabric of American history a splendid record of accomplishments in practically all fields of cultural and religious endeavor. Hardly three centuries after the death of St. Francis (1226), they were to be found at work in many parts of the New World, planting the seeds of civilization among the natives of that vast colonial empire of New Spain, to which the Mother Country was fast bringing European political and ecclesiastical organization.

In his *Columbus and His Predecessors*, Dr. Charles Hallan McCarthy has given us a succinct account of the missionary labors of the Franciscans during the century preceding the discovery of America, and has linked the success of their explorations in the Far East with the forces and influences which brought about the first voyage of Columbus and of the discoverers who followed in his wake.[1] No incident in his life is more familiar to us than the chance visit Columbus and his little son, Diego, paid in January, 1492, to the Franciscan priory of La Rabida, where he found at last a patient and intelligent listener in the Guardian, Father Juan Pérez, who was also the confessor of Queen Isabella of Spain. The following August, as a result of the appeal made by Father Pérez, all the arrangements for the celebrated voyage were completed, all the difficulties overcome, and tradition has it that Columbus and his men knelt that

---
[1] 113–114. Philadelphia, 1912.

morning at the Sanctuary rail to receive Holy Communion from the hands of Father Pérez.[2]

It was but natural to expect that after the return of Columbus, the Franciscans would be among the first to plan the evangelization of the new-found world. They had a tradition and a place in missionary history back to the days of St. Francis himself. For a long time, it was believed that Father Bernard Buil, who was sent to Hispaniola in 1493, on the second voyage of Columbus, as Vicar-Apostolic of the New World, was a Franciscan; but recent researches have connected him with a community called the Order of the Minims of St. Francis, founded by St. Francis of Paula (Calabria), in 1435.[3] When, however, Cardinal Ximénez, himself a Franciscan, became Archbishop of Toledo and Primate of Spain (1495), the missionary activities of the friars began in earnest, and as early as 1505, there were enough members of the Order in the West Indies to warrant the erection of an independent Province, which bore the title of the Holy Cross. Father García of Padilla, a Franciscan, was consecrated first Bishop of San Domingo in 1512, and by the time Hernando Cortés had completed the conquest of Mexico (1519-1521), the Franciscans were to be found in the newly discovered parts of America, and had, indeed, by that date begun the long martyrology which bears so striking and so pathetic a proof of their heroic zeal for the Faith. Cortés appealed to Pope Leo X in 1521 to send members of the religious orders to Mexico, so that the conversion of the natives might be begun in earnest; and the next year, the Emperor, Charles V, sent out three Flemish Franciscans, the best known of whom is Brother Peter of Ghent.[4]

But the work of conversion in Mexico began on a grand scale

---

[2] For the share taken in the enterprise by the members of another great mendicant Order, the Dominicans, cf. Mandonnet, *Les Dominicains et la Découverte de l'Amérique* (Paris, 1893). Both Columbus and Queen Isabella belonged to the Third Order of St. Francis. (Cf. Engelhardt, *Missions and Missionaries in California*, I, 9. San Francisco, 1908).

[3] See the fac-simile of Buil's appointment in the *Catholic Encyclopedia* (I, 414). Cf. Heimbucher, *Die Orden und Kongregationen der kath. Kirche*, II, 527. Paderborn, 1907. Engelhardt (*op. cit.*, Appendix B) has given an explanation of the various theories about Buil. Cf. Ryan, "Diocesan Organization in the Spanish Colonies," in the *Catholic Historical Review*, for July, 1916.

[4] Cf. Cuevas, *Historia de la Iglesia en Mexico*, (I, c. IV ... *Los primeros Misioneros Franciscanos*). Mexico, 1921.

The Coming of the Franciscans to New Spain (1522–1675)

two years later, when the "Twelve Apostles," as the band of Franciscans under the leadership of Fray Martín of Valencia is known, came to the aid of their three Flemish brethren. Engelhardt tells us that soon after reaching the capital (Mexico City), Fray Martin, "who was clothed with the authority of a Vicar-Apostolic, convoked the first ecclesiastical council in the New World. . . . The aim of the friars was to gather the boys into schools connected with the various convents, and then to teach their pupils reading, writing, and singing. Often as many as six or eight hundred children received an elementary education under the same roof. . . . So deep was the impression made by these friars that the arrival of the Franciscans under Father Martín of Valencia became the starting point in the chronology of the natives under the term of: *the year when the faith came.*"[5]

Progress followed so swiftly after the Synod of 1524 that Charles V decided to ask the Holy See to give Mexico episcopal jurisdiction; and on December 12, 1527, the Franciscan, Fray Juan de Zumárraga, was nominated by the Spanish Crown to the diocese of Mexico City, which it was planned to erect immediately. Without waiting for episcopal consecration Bishop-elect Zumárraga set out for New Spain in the autumn of 1528 and reached his See on December 6, of that year. During the next few years he was busily engaged in bringing order and peace into the new Spanish colony; and when everything was arranged to his satisfaction, he returned to Spain (May, 1532), and was consecrated at Valladolid on April 23, 1533. After remaining six months in Spain on matters connected with the welfare of the Indians, Bishop Zumárraga sailed for Mexico, arriving in the episcopal city in October, 1534. From this time on until the reorganization of episcopal jurisdiction in New Spain in 1545, the Franciscans spread the work of their missions far and wide among the natives, building churches, convents, and schools, initiating the Indians into the various trades and handicrafts, and training them in agricultural pursuits.

It is not within the scope of this chapter to describe in detail the Church history of Mexico from the return of Zumárraga until the foundation of the Franciscan missionary colleges

---

[5] Engelhardt, *op. cit.*, I, 12–13. A "custody" was a small province. A picture of the "Twelve Apostles" will be found in Cuevas, *op. cit.*, opposite p. 168.

(Querétaro, Zacatecas, and San Fernando), from which, as from three well organized centers, the friars began their methodic approach into what is now the present state of Texas. It will suffice to note in passing that in 1546 Zumárraga became the first Archbishop of Mexico City, although he did not live long enough to receive the official brief of his election.[6] The Bull of February 11, 1546, creating the suffragan Sees of Oaxaca, Tlaxcala, Michoacan, Guatemala, and Chiapas, did not reach Mexico until late in 1548.

The growth of these suffragan Sees, with others added from time to time by the Popes, especially the Dioceses of Durango (1620), Linares (1777), and Sonora (1779), brought the whole southwestern section of the present United States under the jurisdiction of the archbishop of Mexico City.[7] Back of this growth of diocesan jurisdiction there are many historic pages, glowing with heroic zeal, with trials almost indescribable, and with martyrdoms that outdo the early days of the Christian Faith,—all of which form part of the story of Franciscan effort from the establishment of the Province of the Holy Gospel (1535) to the end of Mexican ecclesiastical jurisdiction in our Hispanic Southwest. There are names in the annals of these years that can never be forgotten, and among them is that of Fray Marcos de Niza, who brought Arizona and New Mexico within the ken of the government of New Spain and who revealed thereby a new and vast territory to the spiritual devotion of his Franciscan brothers. His famous journey of 1539, as Engelhardt points out, occurred "some years before the death of Martin Luther, sixty-eight years before any English colony was founded in the Western hemisphere, and two hundred thirty-seven years before the Declaration of Independence."[8] There is also the name of the Proto-Martyr of the New World, Fray Juan de Padilla, who was put to death, with two of his Franciscan brothers, by the Indians in 1542. From 1539 until the end of the eighteenth century, nearly three hundred Franciscans, of

---

[6] Verelst, *Zumarraga, eerste Bisschop, Aartsbisschop van Mexico*. (Rousselaere, 1907).

[7] Mendieta, *Historia eclesiatica indiana*. (Mexico, 1870). The Bulls for the erection of these Sees will be found in Hernaez, *Colección de Bulas y otros Documentos para la Historia de America*, II, 79-88 (Brussels, 1879).

[8] *Op. cit.*, I, 15. Cf. Engelhardt, *The Franciscans in Arizona*, pp. 20-30. (Harbor Springs, Mich., 1899).

The Coming of the Franciscans to New Spain (1522-1675)

whom thirty-eight were killed by the natives, labored in the southwestern territory of the United States. Our attention is principally directed to those expeditions and explorations which gradually revealed this territory to the Church and State officials of New Spain. In his *Spanish Exploration in the Southwest*, Bolton has published the original narratives of these expeditions in the northern section of the country —one day to become a tier of States in the New Republic—from 1535 to 1706.[9] In all these expeditions and explorations the Franciscans participated.

Although some of the leaders of these expeditions had already set foot on Texan soil, it was not until the danger of a French settlement in 1685 by La Salle threatened Spanish occupation of the country, that the viceroys, Marqués de Laguna (1686), and Conde de Monclova (1687) began active exploration of the province of Texas. Previous to this, they had despatched the Bosque-Larios expedition of 1675 into Texas, and in this journey the Franciscans, Fray Juan Larios and Fray Dionysio de la Buenaventura, accompanied the soldiers. The Mendoza expedition among the Jumano Indians in 1683–1684 had among its leaders Father Nicolás López and other Franciscans, and in the De Leon-Massanet expedition of 1689-1690, Father Massanet, who is some times called the Founder of the Texas Missions, was the chief spiritual authority.

But these three explorations of Texás, while a part of the proximate approach of the Franciscans to the Texas mission field, do not exhaust the whole of Franciscan history in that portion of Spain's vast colonial possessions. All along the years from 1535 to 1675, there were efforts to penetrate the unknown lands of the Texas Indians, and in each of these explorations were found Franciscans, who have written their names high on the scroll of fame. Some of these Franciscans brought back to their superiors more accurate knowledge of the land beyond the Rio Grande. In June, 1581, three friars, Fray Juan de Santa María, Fray Agustín Rodríguez, and Fray Francisco López, started out with Chamuscado and his party of soldiers and Indian servants, and reached the Tiguan towns near Bernalillo, in New Mexico. While not directly of value for the history of

---

[9] New York, 1925.

the approach to Texas, this expedition, in which all three friars lost their lives, had important consequences for Texas Franciscan history, since it was the direct cause of the Espejo expedition in which Fray Bernaldino Beltrán was a leader and which eventually penetrated the territory of the Jumano Indians, near El Paso. These two explorations, while fruitless from the standpoint of permanent settlements, stirred up so much enthusiasm that, even had the French invasion not occurred a century later, it is quite probable that Texas would have been explored and evangelized. Other wealthy citizens of Mexico, among whom were Cristóbal Martín (1583), Francisco Diaz de Vargas (1583), Juan Bautista de Lomas y Colmenares (1589), Gaspar Castaño de Sosa (1590), Francis Leyva de Bonilla and Antonio Guitiérrez de Humaña (1593), attempted to obtain permission to explore the land beyond the Rio Grande. These adventures had the promise of Franciscan aid, but it was not until 1595 that Juan de Oñate received official permission to carry out the plan. With Oñate, when he finally started northward in 1598, was Fray Rodrigo Durán, the Franciscan commissary, and later his successor, Fray Martínez, and a band of missionaries of the same Order. Though Oñate's main interest was to settle the country beyond the river (one hundred thirty of his men had brought along their wives and families), he did not neglect the spiritual problems involved in his great task.

This is evident from his letter to the viceroy, dated March 2, 1599, in which he speaks of Fray Martínez: "To make this request of you, Illustrious Sir, I am sending the best qualified persons I have in my camp, for it is but reasonable that such should go on an errand of such importance to the service of God and his Majesty, in which they risk their health and life, looking lightly upon the great hardships which they must suffer and have suffered. Father Fray Alonso Martínez, apostolic commissary of these provinces of New Mexico, is the most meritorious person with whom I have had any dealings, and of the kind needed by such great kingdoms for their spiritual government. Concerning this I am writing to his Majesty, and I shall be greatly favored if your Lordship shall do the same. I believe your Lordship is under loving obligation to do this, both because the said Father Commissary is your client as well as because of the Authority of his person and of the merits of his worthy life,

The Coming of the Franciscans to New Spain (1522–1675)

of which I am sending to his Majesty a special report, which your Lordship will see if you desire, and to which I refer. In his company goes my cousin, Father Fray Cristóbal de Salazar, concerning whom testimony can be given by his prelates, for in order not to appear an interested witness in my own cause I refrain from saying what I could say with much reason and truth. For in all spiritual matters I refer you to the said fathers, whom I beg your Lordship to credit in every respect as you would credit me in person. I say but little to your Lordship as to your crediting them as true priests of my father St. Francis. With such as these may your Lordship swell these your kingdoms, for there is plenty for them to do."[10]

The approach to Texas was nearer with the success of Oñate's expedition, but the actual advance was not made until 1675, when almost contemporaneously with the Bosque expedition was founded the first of those apostolic missionary colleges from which Texas was at last to receive its permanent missions and missionaries.

By the year 1675, a century and a half had passed since the advent of the "Twelve Apostles." In every town and village permanently settled by the Spanish in New Spain, the Franciscans had established permanent centers of educational and religious life, the Church had witnessed marvelous development in the creation of episcopal Sees, colleges and universities, and all through the "Land of Sunshine" the name of Christ and His Mother was spoken in tender accents of a profound faith by the natives. With a glorious record of success in Mexico proper, it was to be expected that once the Franciscans began to move northward beyond the Rio Grande, the same success would be visible in their work.

---
[10] Cited from Bolton, *Spanish Exploration etc.*, pp. 221–222.

CHAPTER II.

THE APPROACH OF THE MISSIONARIES TO TEXAS (1675-1689).

Chief among the narratives we possess for the period between the Oñate expedition and that by Fernando del Bosque is the celebrated *Memorial* of Fray Alonso de Benavides of 1630.[1] Benavides was appointed first Guardian of the "Custodia de la Conversion de San Pablo," when New Mexico was separated into a special district in 1621. Eight years later he was relieved of this post and was advised to proceed at once to Spain to inform the Spanish Crown of "the most notable things which had transpired in our Holy Custody" of New Mexico. The *Memorial* was the result of this order, and while not directly treating the condition of affairs in those parts of Texas which were then known, it contains many general reflections on the state of the Indians and on the best methods of their conversion. It may be that the Franciscians, when they did begin permanent mission settlements in Texas before the end of the century, followed the advice and suggestions contained in the *Memorial*. One direct link between Benavides and Fray Massanet is the tradition the latter found among the Hasinai Indians of the "presence" of Madre María de Jesús de Agreda.[2]

Benavides may be considered as belonging particularly to this period of Texas, for his *Memorial* reveals the fact that he was one of the earliest among the Franciscans to look with longing eyes toward the missionary development of Texas. In his *Memorial*, he records the hope that the king of Spain would open a port of entry on the Gulf Coast "between the Cape of Apalache and the coast of Tampico," so that the friars might have a base or headquarters for their proposed work in Texas.

---
[1] Printed with English translation by Mrs. Edward E. Ayer (New York, 1916). It is one of the scarcest of all Americana. For discussion of value of Ayer copy, cf. "The Benavides Memorials," by J. P. O'Hara, in the *Catholic Historical Review* (I, 76-78). In the Guilday Transcripts there is a second *Memorial* (dated 1634), probably more authentic than the Ayer copy.

[2] For a careful account of this strange phenomenon, cf. Ayer, *op. cit.*, p. 277.

His own words are explicit: "So that if this port or bay of Espíritu Santo were settled up, there would be saved in that direction more than eight hundred leagues, which are the (distance) from New Mexico to the Havana, coming by (way of) Mexico. The which (leagues) are travelled in more than a year; and four hundred of them through a land of war very perilous, where your majesty makes many expenditures in escorts of soldiers, and (in) wagons. And this way from the bay of Espíritu Santo all this is saved in only a hundred leagues of road, which is the (distance) from the Kingdom of Quivira to this bay. And all the road (is) pacific, of friendly and known people, who today must be converted and must be conferring about their baptism; for in this state I left them the year past. . . . From there (one) can with facility, in light vessels, trade and traffic with all the coast of New Spain, Tampico, San Juan de Lua (San Juan de Ulua), Campeche, Havana, and Florida, and all in sight of land . . . on all that coast, clear to Florida, there are (tiene) much pearls, and amber; and today they are all lost by the (locality) not being settled. And for this reason so many hostile Hollanders roam there, robbing whatsoever light vessels cross the gulf. And if the Bay were settled, they would not have anywhere to take refuge. Even so, to carry from Mexico to New Mexico all the necessaries which your majesty sends to these churches, one goes through five hundred leagues, and most of them at war, and then, to reach Quivira, it is necessary to travel another one hundred and fifty (leagues) in which Your Majesty will pay more than the principal is worth. And all this is saved (by) sending it in a light vessel from the Havana to the bay of Espíritu Santo, if (that) is settled up.[3]

The march from New Mexico toward the east and the south was a steady one, and it is not difficult to trace in such sources as the *Memorial* the gradual approach of the friars to their new field of missionary labor. In one place, Benavides tells us, after recounting the glories of the New Mexican missions: "For all, God be infinitely praised. From the (aforesaid) may well be inferred the so copious spiritual blessings which our seraphic Order (Religion) hath discovered throughout all the new world. And in this region it alone is (the Order) which with so great travails and risks makes these so superb discoveries. Since, as

---
[3] Benavides, *Memorial*, p. 65.

has been said, in (one) sole stretch of one hundred leagues it has baptized more than eight thousand souls, and built more than fifty very beautiful churches and monasteries. And they are more than five hundred thousand Indians those whom we have pacific and subject to your Majesty in all the neighboring nations, who are little by little being catechised to be baptized. In such sort that though all that territory belonged to the Demon until now, and was thick with idolatry, without there being a person to praise the Most Holy Name of Jesus, today it is all thick with temples and monasteries and with pedestals of the Cross; and there is no one that does not praise God and His Most Holy Mother aloud in the wilds when they are saluting one another."[4]

The spiritual sons of the Poor Little Man of Assisi, with their more than fifty churches and monasteries in New Mexico, were journeying nearer and nearer to Texas. And how beautifully is manifested their devotion to the spirit of their saintly Founder! Numerous Indians were being prepared for Baptism. The Most Holy Names of Jesus, and of His Most Holy Mother were being praised aloud in the wilds, and crosses marked the skyline. The devotion to the Most Holy Name, the devotion to the Sacred Passion of Our Divine Lord, and devotion to the Blessed Virgin Mary, were fervent in the hearts of the Franciscans. These devotions mean so much in Catholic life and religious practice that a debt of gratitude is due to the sons of St. Francis for establishing them so early in the religious annals of the western world.

The particular point of interest to us is that these devotions (and the religious truths which are their foundation) were being taught to tribes of Indians among whom were the Jumano nation whose habitat was "a hundred and twelve leagues to the east" of Santa Fé. Father Juan de Salas was the first Franciscan to be sent to answer the plea of these Indians for Baptism and religious instruction. In 1629, Salas and Father Juan Diego López, with Indians as guides, set out for the region of the Jumano. In her excellent monograph—*The Beginnings of Spanish Settlement in the El Paso District*—Anne E. Hughes places the region of the Jumanos in western Texas near the Colorado

[4] *Ibid.*, p. 62.

River (Rio de las Nueces).[5] The two padres and the three soldiers accompanying them were taken by surprise on arriving at the place of the Jumano who came forth in procession to meet them, bearing two crosses in the front of the rank. The fathers took their crucifixes from their necks and the Jumanos came to kiss and to venerate the image of the crucified Saviour. Father Benavides relates how devotedly they put their lips on "a very pretty Infant Jesus that they (the Padres) carried." More than ten thousand souls assembled on that field in west Texas to hear Father Salas preach the word of the Lord. Father Salas asked them if they desired with all their hearts to be baptized. The captains of the people responded that that desire had brought them together and for that alone they had summoned the friars. But Father Salas desired further assurance. He asked that all those who wished to become Christians to raise the arm. All arms went up, even those of the suckling babes were raised by the mothers. By so touching a scene the Fathers were moved to compassion and remained there some few days to preach the divine word and to teach the Jumano how to pray. Morning and evening they crowded around. The fame of this event quickly spread to the neighboring nations, and from them came messengers to beg the like administrations. But the harvest was great and the laborers were few and the Franciscans returned to seek aid from their superiors. But before saying farewell Father Salas exhorted them to come daily before a cross, erected there by themselves, and to pray until he should return. But the chief captain of the Jumano had a special request to make before the Father's departure. Coming to Father Salas, the commissary of the journey, he said: "Padre, we can not yet do anything with God, for we are like deer and animals of the wilds; and thou canst (do) much with God and this holy Cross. And we have many sick ones—cure them first (before) that thou goest."[6]

Between the first journey of Father Juan de Salas into what is now western central Texas in 1629 and the Bosque expedition of 1675, several attempts were made by the Franciscans to penetrate eastward from the El Paso district. In 1650, Captain

---

[5] Published in *Studies in American History*, University of California Publications in History, I, 295–392 (1914).
[6] Benavides, *Memorial*, p. 61.

Hernando Martín and Diego del Castillo are said to have been the first to meet natives from the kingdom of Texas. No mention is made of any friars being part of the company of these adventurers. But during the quarter-century separating the last-named expedition from that of Fernando del Bosque in 1675, the missionary work in and around El Paso continued to flourish. The mission of Nuestra Señora de Guadalupe, which was founded in 1659, the mission of San Francisco, twelve leagues below Guadalupe, and La Soledad, seventy leagues to the southeast of Guadalupe, were all centers of Spanish life with a fully organized Franciscan missionary system. Nuestra Señora de Guadalupe owes its foundation to the friars, Fray García de San Francisco y Zúñiga and Fray Francisco de Salazar.[7]

Few names have greater prominence in Texas Catholic history than that of Father García. His work, as Hughes points out, "may be regarded as the cornerstone of the El Paso establishments."[8] A certified copy of the narrative of the founding of Nuestra Señora de Guadalupe still exists in the archives of the Church of Guadalupe at Júarez, and is as follows:

> In the name of the most holy and indivisible Trinity, Father, Son, and Holy Ghost, three distinct persons and one only true God; for his greater glory, honor, and reverence; for the confusion of the infernal enemy; for the service of the most holy Virgin Mary; our Lady and immaculate Patron; and for the greater exaltation of our Holy Catholic faith; on the eighth day of the month of December, of the year 1659, I, Fray Garcia de San Francisco of the order of the minor friars of the regular observance of our Seraphic Father San Francisco, preacher, actual difinitor of the holy custody of the conversion of San Pablo of New Mexico, minister and guardian of the convent of San Antonio del Pueblo de Senecú: whereas the captains and old men of the heathendom of the Mansos and Zumanas Indians went to the said custody to supplicate me to descend to preach them the Holy Evangel of Our Lord Jesus Christ and succeed in quieting them and baptizing them; and our Reverend Father Fray Juan Gonsales, custodian of said custody, having given a patent to Señor Don Juan, Manso governor and captain-general for his majesty; and having received the patents from my superior, in which he orders me to descend for the instruction and conversion of this heathendom, and license from the said Señor Don Juan, Manso governor; and having

---
[7] Hughes, *op. cit.*, p. 305.
[8] *Ibid.*

descended with no little labor, to El Passo del Rio del Norte, on the border of New Spain, and in the middle of the custody and province of New Mexico; and having congregated most of the rancherías of the Manso heathen on said site; and having offered them the evangelical word, and they having accepted it for their catechism, and permitted me to build a little church of branches and mud and a monastery thatched with straw—said heathen aiding and receiving me for their preacher and minister; by these acts as aforesaid, and by virtue of the patent of apostolic commissary, which I have from my superiors, through the privileges which the apostolic chair has displayed for new conversions to our sacred religion, raising this holy cross, which I planted, and building this church, in which already I have celebrated the sacred mystery of our redemption, I took possession of this conversion of the Mansos and Sumanas, and of the other surrounding heathen which might be assembled or might be called to our or to whatever evangelical preacher, in name of all our sacred religion, and immediately of the custody of the conversion of San Pablo of New Mexico; and I named and dedicated this holy church and conversion to the most holy Virgin of Guadalupe with the above name of El Passo, placing (as I do place) her holy image, for the which and to redeem it from the demon's tyrannical possession, I call to witness heaven, the earth, and all the holy angels who are present as guard, and especially all the heathen who are of this conversion, and Bernadino Gualtoye, Antonio Guilixigue, Antonio Elogua, Juan Azoloye, Francisco Tzitza, and Felipe Quele, Christians of the Pueblo of Senecú, companions and followers who descended with me.

And as soon as I named this conversion, by the authority of my office, as commissary and head of all these of El Rio del Norte above and surrounding immediately subject to the holy custody of the conversion of San Pablo, and in order that in future times thus it may be confirmed of this possession, dedication, and naming, I write this in order that it may be preserved in the archive of said holy custody. Dated at El Rio del Norte, at the pass from New Spain to New Mexico, on the 8th day of December, 1659.

Fray Garcia de San Francisco, Apostolic Commissary of the Mansos and Zumanas—I, Fray Antonio Tabares, notary named by Father Fray Garcia de San Francisco, Apostolic Commissary of these conversions, testify to having transcribed, as above, the said writing, which is preserved in the archive of the custody. Dated April 9, 1663; and as true I sign it.[9]

---

[9] *Op. cit.*, p. 306 (Printed from the Bandelier Collection, Harvard University).

Father García's ministry in the El Paso missions extended over a term of twelve years (1659-1671), and his life and works are recorded by contemporary historians and chroniclers.[10] The occupation of the El Paso district by the Spanish settlers coincides with the founding of these three missions, the two latter, however, being on the Mexican side of the Rio Grande del Norte. The first marriage record of El Paso is dated November 29, 1678.

Hughes gives us a succinct account of the Franciscan priests who labored in this part of Texas:

> The importance of the missionary center may be gathered from the number of priests present in the monastery during the first two decades of its existence. From the old church records at Júarez, it is learned that before 1680 fourteen priests had been at the mission during periods of varying lengths—these not including the names of Father Francisco de Salazar and Fray Antonio Tabares, the assistants of Father García mentioned above. Benito de la Natividad was there during eight years of García's guardianship. The name of Fray Juan Alvarez appears in 1667, Fray José de Truxillo in 1668, and Fray Agustín de Santa María, Fray Sebastian Navorro, and Fray Nicolás de Salazar in 1675. Of these only Fray Agustín seems to have remained in El Paso very long. Fray Juan de Bonilla, the probable successor of García, had charge of the mission in 1677, when Father Francisco de Ayeta, "Custodia y Júez Eclesiastico de los Conberziones de San Pedro y Pablo de Nuebo Mexico," accompanied by his secretary, Fray Antonio de Sierra, made his first *visita* on October 10. In 1667 Fray Nicolas de Echavarría joined Father Bonilla, and they both served under Father Alvarez, who was guardian until 1679. On July 3, 1680, Ayeta made his second *visita*, accompanied by a new secretary, Father Fray Pedro Gómez de San Antonio, who later became guardian and served at the mission for forty years. Fray Nicolas Hurtado's name occurs in the records of 1672, and then is not mentioned for several years; later he succeeded Ayeta as custodian, Fray Pedro Gómez serving as his secretary. Fray José Valdez came to Guadalupe in 1680.

Judged by the records, the efforts of these missionaries were not remarkably successful. The following statistics indicate the extent of the conversions. Before 1680 they had baptized eight hundred and thirty Mansos—if the Indians whose tribal affiliation was not given were Mansos—

---

[10] Cf. Vetancurt, *Menologio Franciscano de los Varones mas señalados* (Mexico, 1697); Medina, *Chronica de la Santa Provincia de San Diego de Mexico* (Mexico, 1682).

Approach to Texas 15

sixty-two Piros, seventeen Sumas, ten Tanos, five Apaches, and four Jumanos. The statistics of certain years are significant. From July 16, 1662, to April 1, 1663, about twenty-four Indians were baptized; between April 1, 1663, and about April 1, 1664, over three hundred Indians, chiefly adults; during 1663, the most prosperous year before September 20, 1680, two hundred and seventy-six Indians, mostly older children and adults; in 1668, only three Mansos; in 1679, seventy-one Mansos, fourteen Piros, six Sumas, two Jumanos, and two Tanos. The tribe to which the Indians belonged was not indicated in early years; after 1667 the name of Piros, Jumanos, and other tribal affiliations was not taken until Father Echavarría took charge in October, 1677.[11]

For over twenty-five years, the El Paso district had witnessed an incredible activity on the part of these Franciscan missionaries, who carried the tidings of the Gospel to many native Indian tribes, including the Mansos, Sumas, Tanos, Jumanos, Piros, and Tiguas. Some fourteen Indian Pueblos were built in this period and each of these pueblos had a church with a resident or visiting priest. This fact must be kept in mind when we come to the great work of Father Massanet in 1690 in Eastern Texas; for, without depriving him of the honor of being called the Founder of the Texas Missions, the "true beginnings of what is now Texas are to be found in the settlements grouped along the Rio del Norte in the El Paso District."[12]

Meanwhile, the approach into Texas was being made in another section of the province. The first of these attempts is centered around the name of Fray Juan Larios, a Franciscan of the Province of Santiago de Jalisco, whose central convent was at Guadalajara. In 1670, Father Larios visited the Indians of the Coahuila district and of the region north of the Rio Grande, and in 1673 went again to those parts, accompanied by two other Franciscans, Fray Juan Dionysio de Penasco and a lay brother, Manuel de la Cruz. The following year, Larios, Manuel, and Fray Dionysio de San Buenaventura, a new volunteer among the missionaries, again penetrated into Texas.[13] This expedition was placed in charge of Fernando del Bosque in 1675 and it can be considered the first systematic exploration of Texas from the

---
[11] *Op. cit.*, pp. 313–314.
[12] *Ibid.*, p. 392.
[13] Cf. Bolton, "The Spanish Occupation of Texas (1519–1690)," in the *Southwestern Historical Quarterly* (XVI, 11–17).

east central section "The Bosque-Larios expedition across the Rio Grande," writes Bolton, "though not great in size or extent, was important in its bearings. Taken with the preliminary reconnaisance of Fray Manuel de la Cruz a few months before, it is the earliest well-authenticated missionary expedition on record to cross the Rio Grande from the south at any point below the Pecos. Bosque's report on the Indian situation is one of the most valuable extant for the region and period. As a result of the reports and recommendations of Bosque and Father Larios, four missions were soon established in the Coahuila district, to serve Indians living to the north as well as to the south of the Rio Grande. And now the Tejas, Indians living far on the Louisiana border, rose above the Coahuila horizon. In 1676 the Bishop of Guadalajara visited Monclova, and one of the reasons which he gave for favoring the adoption of the measures urged by Bosque was the opportunity it would afford to reach and convert the more important Tejas, beyond."[14]

The next expedition into Texas for which there is authentic historical evidence was organized in 1683 with Captain Juan Domínguez de Mendoza, who was accompanied by the Franciscans, Fray López and Fray Zavaleta. It resulted in the effort made by the two Franciscans, after their return in 1685 and in 1686, to induce the Spanish officials to settle the Jumano country with permanent missionaries and soldiers. Bolton is of the opinion that "it is not at all improbable that if danger from the French on the Gulf coast had not just arisen, the recommendations would have been put into effect."[15]

William Edward Dunn has described in his *Spanish and French Rivalry in the Gulf Region of the United States (1672–1702)* the actual beginning of Spanish colonization in the present State of Texas.[16] A swift dramatic episode, fraught with great possibilities, occurred when La Salle landed in February, 1685, at Matagorda Bay (Bay St. Louis), with a royal commission to conquer and to govern that portion of North America lying between Fort St. Louis on the Illinois River and the Gulf of Mexico. Rumors of a French invasion of Quivira and Teguayo had been rife since the revelation of Pensacola scheme in

---

[14] *Spanish Exploration* etc., p. 288.
[15] *Ibid.*, p. 317.
[16] Published in *Studies in History*, No. I, of the University of Texas *Bulletin* (January, 1917).

Approach to Texas

1678. "While Spain slumbered," writes Dunn, "French explorers had been preparing the way for the extension of the sovereignty of France over the great interior region of the Mississippi Valley. The high-water mark of French enterprise was reached in 1682, when La Salle descended the Mississippi to its mouth, and took possession in the name of Louis XIV of the vast territory drained by its waters."[17] The following year Spain and France were at war, and the 1684-85 expedition may be considered as part of the hostilities.

Our immediate interest in La Salle's invasion of Texas and in his erection of Fort St. Louis lies in the fact that he was accompanied by three Franciscans: Father Zenobius Membré, who had been La Salle's companion on the voyage of discovery in 1682; Father Anastasius Douay, and Father Maximus Le Clercq. The whole project met with disaster after disaster. La Salle himself was murdered by one of his own men (January, 1687), while the Indians wiped out the fort.

Spain was at last aroused to the danger of French invasion into her colonies from the east and with the expedition of Captain Alonso de León, who was accompanied by Fray Damian Massanet, in 1689, Texas was opened to Spanish colonization; and by means of the knowledge Father Massanet acquired from the Texas Indians, the difficulties surrounding the approach to the vast province across the Rio Grande were finally solved and the road was cleared for the soldiers of the Cross who were to come in such great numbers for the next century.

The De León-Massanet expedition was more successful than any of its predecessors. It gave the Spanish officials the assurance that the French danger had passed. It "quickened their religious zeal, and caused them to be imbued with a spirit of gratitude to the Almighty for the renewed proof of His divine aid and favor. In this pious atmosphere, the plans that had been conceived by the leaders of the recent expedition for the extension of the Gospel into the newly-discovered region in the north were to meet with prompt and hearty approval."[18] It was natural that the new mission field should be assigned to the recently erected Apostolic College of the Holy Cross at Querétaro.

---
[17] *Op. cit.*, p. 31.
[18] *Ibid.*, p. 110.

CHAPTER III.

The Querétaran Missions—I: (1690–1731).

The growing activity of the Franciscans in the mission field of northern New Spain received a permanent organization in the establishment of three apostolic colleges, where volunteers for the Indian missions, priests and lay brothers, were educated in a methodical way for their arduous and complicated work. These colleges, as Engelhardt has written, were independent houses of study, subject directly to the Franciscan Commissary-General for the Indies, whose residence was at Madrid.[1]

The first of these in point of time is the Apostolic College of Querétaro, Mexico, founded by Pope Innocent XI, on May 8, 1683. The second is the College of Nuestra Señora de Guadalupe at Zacatecas, Mexico, erected by the Venerable Fray Antonio de Margil, in 1706. The third is the College of San Fernando in Mexico City, established by Pope Clement XII, in 1734.

The Franciscan missionaries who were trained in these apostolic colleges are usually known as Querétaranos, Zacatecanos, and Fernandinos. To the priests and lay-brothers of these three central houses can be traced practically all the mission settlements in what is now the State of Texas. The Bull *Sacrosancti Apostolatus* of May 8, 1682, forms the basic constitution of these three colleges. It lays down in detail the method of their erection, their daily curriculum, the type of missioner to be chosen, and the regulations governing their work among the Indians. Over each College was a guardian and four councillors (*discrétos*). These latter were elected every four years by the community; the guardian was chosen from a *terna* sent to the Commissary-General by the Chapter of the College. Hernaez in his *Coleccion de Bulas etc.*, has not printed the *Sacrosancti Apostolatus*, but Engelhardt has given us an analysis of this important document from Parras' *Gobierno de los Regulares de la America*.[2] Engelhardt writes:

> The guardian, with the consent of the discretos, could admit any friar, cleric, or lay-brother, from any of the prov-

---
[1] *Op. cit.*, I, 615.
[2] Published, 2 vols., in Madrid, 1783.

inces, provided the applicant, after due examination as to health, virtue and studies was judged suitable and worthy by the discretos; nor could anyone except the commissary-general prevent his admission. A novitiate was attached to the College, into which suitable young men were received and where they were trained by one of the Fathers who was elected at the chapter and bore the title of master of novices. The community at the College was never to consist of more than thirty friars, of whom twenty-six were to be priests and four lay-brothers. The latter attended to housework and the collecting of alms.

Inasmuch as these monasteries were to excel in spirituality and self-denial, the Papal Bull expressly directed that in said seminary the Rule of the Friars Minor should be most strictly observed, as well in regard to poverty in general as in regard to the special regulations concerning the quality and number of wearing apparel, going barefooted, fasting, etc., particularly with regard to providing the necessaries for the friars in sickness and in health according to our mode of life, so that all live in community, and that in no case any friar shall be permitted to have, neither in charge of the apostolic syndic nor in charge of spiritual friends whosoever the owner may be, any money deposits for his own necessities.

That indispensably every day they shall devote two hours to mental prayer, one in the morning and one in the evening. The Divine Office shall be recited in choir at stated hours . . . at which and at the conventual Mass, and at the other community exercises all without exception shall be bound to be present. (Matins and Lauds were chanted at midnight.)

That every day for two hours there shall be lectures and conferences for one hour after the conventual Mass on the Language of the Indians, and for one hour after Vespers on the manner of converting, teaching catechism, and instructing converts. No one shall be excused from attending these lectures, nor from giving account on the subject of the lecture if he be questioned.

That no secular person shall be permitted to enter the interior parts of the convent, but in the outer cloister a decent and edifying room containing a few plain seats, shall be set apart, where male seculars desiring to speak with any of the Fathers for their consolation may be received and comforted.

That the guardian, or in his absence, the presiding Father, on suitable occasions, or when he deems it necessary, shall send out missionaries by twos, or in larger numbers, as it shall seem expedient for the conversion of the people, assigning to them the villages, districts, and territories in which the several religious may preach their missions. Some, however, shall be left at the seminary to carry on the exercises of the community, and these may be sent out when the others return.

That if any of the missionaries without legitimate cause, which must be approved by the discretos, shall have excused himself from preaching the missions according to the regulation of the Fr. Guardian, or if in the missions he shall have accepted anything beyond moderate food, or shall have given bad example, or in the seminary shall have disturbed the peace of the community, or in attending the community and other exercises to be observed as said before shall have been notably negligent, and if reproved once and again by the guardian shall not have improved, the guardian himself, with the counsel and consent of the discretos, may, if he had been a member of a province, expel him from the seminary and return him to his province, which shall be obliged to receive him back.

That the said commissary-general shall be bound, either personally or through his commissary especially appointed for that purpose, to visit said seminary every three years, and at each visitation he shall question each one about the observance of all aforesaid regulations. . . . And inasmuch as we hope that, inspired by the grace of God, by means of these ministers of His Word, many pagan nations will be converted to the faith, whose neophytes it is necessary to preserve in the faith embraced and to administer to them the sacraments, it is ordered that some of the said missionaries, who are necessary to perform said work, shall remain among the converted people, after they have notified the guardian of the seminary and received permission from him, and they shall always remain subordinate to the same guardian and subject to correction from him, as above. . . . They may remain in charge of souls thus converted to the faith only so long until it shall have pleased the bishop, to whom the territory pertains, or in the future may pertain, to assign secular priests to whom he may commit the care of the souls. (In cura animarum sic conversarum ad fidem, tamdiu solummodo poterunt remanere, quoadusque Episcopo, ad quem terra pertinet, vel in posterum pertinebat, placuerit Presbyteros Saeculares, quibus animarum curam committat, destinare.) While, however, the said missionaries shall continue in said charge, they can accept nothing on the title of curates or missionaries, but must live strictly upon the alms obtained by begging or otherwise offered.[3]

---

[3] *Missions and Missionaries of California*, I, 615.

The Querétaran Missions—I: (1690–1731)

There are several ways of listing the missions founded in Texas by the professed fathers and brothers of these three Franciscan colleges. In his *Missionary Labors of the Franciscans among the Indians of the Early Days*,[4] Engelhardt has described twenty-one missions which have been classified as follows:

Group I—among the Hasinai Texans proper in northeast corner of Houston and southwest corner of Cherokee Counties comprising:
1. San Francisco de los Texas.
2. Santísimo Nombre de María.
3. San José de los Nazones.

Group II—comprising:
1. Guadalupe, now Nacogdoches, Texas.
2. Dolores, now San Augustine, Texas.
3. San Miguel, now Robeline, Louisiana.

Group III—at and near the City of San Antonio, Texas, comprising:
1. San Antonio de Valero.
2. Purisima Concepción.
3. San José de Aguayo.
4. San Francisco de la Espada.
5. San Juan Capistrano.

Group IV—in Victoria and Goliad Counties on the Lower Guadalupe and San Antonio Rivers, comprising:
1. Espíritu Santo.
2. Rosário.
3. Refugio, near the junction of the two rivers.

Group V—in Milam County and known as the San Xavier Missions, comprising:
1. Dolores or San Francisco Xavier.
2. Candelaria.
3. San Ildefonso.

Group VI—among the Apache Indians in Menard County on the San Sabá River, comprising:
1. Santa Cruz.
2. San Lorenzo.
3. Candelaria.

Group VII—among the Orcoquiza Indians on the lower Trinity River, De la Luz.

---
[4] Published in *Franciscan Herald* (Chicago), October, 1914—November, 1917.

The Franciscan Missions in Texas

Chronologically the missions established in Texas may be listed as follows:

1. San Francisco de los Texas (1690).
2. Santísimo Nombre de María (1690).
3. San Francisco de los Neches (1716).
4. Purísima Concepción (1716).
5. San José de los Nazones (1716).
6. Nuestra Señora de Guadalupe (1716) at Nacogdoches.
7. Nuestra Señora de los Dolores (1717) at San Augustine.
8. San Miguel (1717) at Robeline, La.
9. San Antonio de Valero (1718).
10. San José de Aguayo (1720).
11. San Xavier de Náxera (1722).
12. Espíritu Santo (1722).
13. Purísima Concepción (1731).
14. San Francisco de la Espada (1731).
15. San Juan Capsitrano (1731).
16. San Francisco Xavier (1746).
17. San Ildefonso (1749).
18. Candelaria (1749).
19. Nuestra Señora del Rosário (1754).
20. San Marcos (1755).
21. Nuestra Señora de la Luz (1756).
22. Nuestra Señora de Guadalupe (1757).
23. Santa Cruz or San Sabá (1757).
24. San Lorenzo (1762).
25. Nuestra Señora del Refugio (1793).

The grouping followed in this and the two succeeding chapters places the Texas missions into a third division; namely, that of the Colleges from which these Franciscans came. This division has the advantage of bringing out into relief the comparative activities of the three groups of missionaries.

The Colegio de la Santa Cruz de Querétaro, founded in 1683, bore the further title *de Propaganda Fide*, and as such has a place in history side by side with the famous Collegio Urbano, established in 1622, in Rome, by the Sacred Congregation de Propaganda Fide for the purpose of sending missionaries to all parts of the world. Querétaro has one of the richest archives for the early history of the Southwest.[5] The story of the Querétaran missions has been told by two of the Fathers of the

---
[5] Bolton, *Guide to Materials for American History in Mexican Archives*, p. 387, Washington, D. C., 1915.

College—Father Isidro Felix Espinosa in his *Chrónica Apostólica y Seráfica de Todos de los Colegios de Propaganda Fide de Esta Neuva-España*, Mexico, 1746, and by Father Juan Domingo Arricivita in his *Crónica Seráfica y Apostólica del Colegio de Propaganda Fide de la Santa Cruz de Querétaro* (Mexico, 1792).[6]

1. San Francisco de los Texas (1690).

On Tuesday of Easter week (March 28, 1690), the little group of Querétarans who accompanied Father Massanet on his journey into Texas, left Coahuila and reached their destination late in May of that year. On June 1, the church which they named in honor of St. Francis was dedicated and thus was begun the first permanent mission in Eastern Texas.[7] The site of the Mission of St. Francis de los Texas is not known, but Bolton has concluded as a result of his own researches, that it was somewhere in the northeastern part of Houston County, northeast of Weches, almost six or seven miles west of the Neches River in the valley of San Pedro Creek.

The narrative of the foundation is given in Father Massanet's letter to the Viceroy as follows: "There came also to that spot an Indian who was thoroughly acquainted with the road into the country of the Tejas, and he showed us the way until we met with the governor of the Tejas, together with fourteen or fifteen of his Indians, and the Indian whom we had sent to him with our message. It was about ten o'clock in the morning when we came upon them by an arroyo in which they were bathing, and, on account of the thick woods, they did not see us until we were very close to them. As soon as the governor saw me he came forward to embrace me; we sat down to talk by signs—this being the most usual mode of communication in those regions; and he produced a small sack of powdered tobacco, of the kind which they grow, and another small sack of *pinole*, white, and of very

---

[6] Copies of these two rare works are in the Library of Congress.

[7] "Saturday, the 27th; Sunday, the 28th; Monday, the 29th; Tuesday, the 30th; and Wednesday, the 31st, they labored to build the church and the dwelling of the apostolic fathers, in the midst of the principal settlement of the Texans. Thursday, June 1st, I gave possession of the said mission, the reverend father commissary, Fray Damian Masanet, having sung Mass in the said church, the said Indian governor and his people attending Mass and the blessing of the church." *Itinerary of De León*, in Bolton, *Spanish Explorations etc.*, p. 417.

good quality. After talking we left the place, and went to rest awhile. That night it was arranged to provide the governor with garments, in order that he might enter his village clothed, so that his people might see how highly we thought of him.

"Three days later, on Monday, May 22, 1690, we entered the village. It was raining on our arrival. That year, it had, up to that time, rained but little, and already the corn was suffering from the drought, but every day of the eleven that we spent in the village it rained very hard.

"At evening on the day of our arrival, the governor being in the tent with us, an old woman brought him for his meal a large earthenware vessel full of cooked frijoles, with ground-nuts and tamales. That evening the governor said that he would spend that night with us in the tent, and take us to his house next day, but afterwards, it being already late, Captain León insisted that they should go at once, as he had some skirts, and other articles of clothing which he wanted to take to the governor's wife. The governor replied that he did not want to go then, but would go next day; however, in spite of all, he was obliged against his will to take León to his house.

"On the next day the governor said that he wished to take us home with him, and that we might live in his house, in which, he said, there was room for all. After dinner we, the priests, discussed what should be our conduct on visiting the governor, and whether it would be advisable to stay there. My opinion was that we four priests should go on foot, carrying our staffs, which bore a holy crucifix, and singing the Litany of Our Lady, and that a lay-brother who was with us should carry in front a picture on linen of the Blessed Virgin, bearing it high on his lance, after the fashion of a banner.

"We set out in this manner for the governor's house from the place where we had stopped, and this pious conduct proved so blessed that although it had rained heavily, and the water stood high all along the road where we had to pass, so high, indeed, that for the greater part of the way it came nearly to our knees, yet our fervor was such that we paid no attention to the water. Following the example given, some of the soldiers who were walking through the water became animated with such zeal and ardor that they could not keep back tears of joy and gladness. Among these who thus especially exerted themselves, giving no heed to the water or to the mud, were Captain Francisco Martínez, Don Gregorio Salinas, and others. The rest, some twenty soldiers, were on horseback, and Captain Alonso de León was with them; we who walked were in their midst.

"We came to the governor's house, where we found a number of Indians—men, women, and children. Kneeling, we concluded the Litany, and we blessed the house. Soon the governor and the other Indians came up to kiss my robe, and the former bade us enter, in order to look at his house. The house is built of stakes thatched over with grass, it is about twenty *varas* high, is round, and has no windows, daylight entering through the door only; this door is like a room-door such as we have here. In the middle of the house is the fire, which is never extinguished by day or by night, and over the door on the inner side there is a little superstructure of rafters very prettily arranged. Ranged around one-half of the house, inside, are ten beds, which consist of a rug made of reeds, laid on four forked sticks. Over the rug they spread buffalo skins, on which they sleep.

"As to whether the priests should live in the governor's house, it seemed to me unadvisable that they should do so, on account of the number of Indians, men and women, who went in and out at all times. Using the Frenchman as an interpreter I told the governor with many kind expressions that his house was very fine, and that I heartily appreciated his desire to have the priests in his household, but that since we had to build a house for the celebration of masses, it might be well to build likewise a dwelling for the priests, because they must needs live near the church. Thereupon the governor said that we should build the house in the most suitable place, that he would show us the village, and that I might choose the spot. We agreed to visit the village on the following day in order to look for a favorable location for the church and the priests' dwelling; accordingly, next day we went with the governor, who took us to the place the French had selected for their settlement, pleasantly and favorably situated on the river banks. We did not locate the convent there because it was so far out of the way of the Indians. Just at that spot they showed us two dead bodies of Frenchmen who had shot each other with carbines. All this day we were unable to find a place which suited me.

"The next morning I went out with Captain Alonso de León

a little way, and found a delightful spot close to the brook, fine woods, with plum trees like those in Spain. And soon afterwards, on the same day, they began to fell trees and cart wood, and within three days we had a roomy dwelling and a church wherein to say Mass with all propriety. We set in front of the church a very high cross of carved wood.

"On the feast of Corpus Christi Mass was sung, and before Mass we had a procession with the holy sacrament exposed, and a large concourse of Indians being assembled, for we had notified them the day before. The soldiers had been given leave to fire as many salutes as they could during the procession, at the elevation, and at the close of Mass, and by the will of the Divine Majesty we celebrated in that solitude a memorable feast, which was rendered a source of great consolation by our being able to carry the blessed sacrament exposed and to walk in procession as Christian Catholics are wont to do. After Mass we hoisted in the name of His Majesty the royal standard bearing on one side the picture of Christ crucified, and on the other that of the Virgin of Guadalupe. A royal salute was fired and we sang the *Te Deum Laudamus* in thanksgiving. . . . They (the Indians) never sacrificed to idols, but only to Him of whom they said that He has all power and that from Him come all things, who is recognized as first cause. . . .

"When the church and the dwelling intended for the priests had been finished they carried into these buildings all that was to be left for the priests, and on the morning of the first of June, the octave of the feast of Corpus Christi, we consecrated the church and celebrated Mass, after which the *Te Deum Laudamus* was sung in thanksgiving, the soldiers firing a royal salute. The church and village were dedicated to Our Holy Father St. Francis. . . . With the priests who were to accompany me, I awaited him (Captain Martínez at the college of the Holy Cross at Querétaro). These priests were the Father Predicador Fray Miguel Fontecuberta, the Father Predicador Fray Francisco de Jesús María, the Father Predicador Fray Antonio Perea, the Father Predicador Fray Francisco Hidalgo, the Father Predicador Fray Antonio Bordoy. Those who remained in the Mission San Salvador were the fathers Fray Antonio Perea and Fray Francisco Hidalgo."[8]

---

[8] Cited in the *Spanish Explorations etc.*, pp. 376–368.

After seeing the mission permanently established and the work of conversion among the Indians begun, Father Massanet placed this first Texas church under the care of the Franciscans who had accompanied him and set out for Mexico City to report to the Viceroy, Gaspar de Galve. A council was held and after listening to Massanet's report, it was determined to send another missionary expedition into Texas. Don Domingo Terán de los Ríos, the governor of Coahuila, was put in charge as commander, and Massanet was directed to select five other Querétarans for the task. The political aspect of the Terán expedition need not be described, since it has little bearing on our subject. The Franciscans selected for the expedition were: Fathers Francisco Hidalgo, Nicolás Prevo, Miguel Estela, Pedro Fortuni, Pedro García, Ildefonso Monge, José Saldana, Antonio Miranda, and Juan de Garaicoechea. Three "donados" or secular Tertiaries also accompanied the fathers.[9]

They set out in May, 1691, and June 18, met some Indians who gave Massanet alarming news of the San Francisco Mission. After some unavoidable delays, they arrived at the mission on August 2, and Massanet found that only two of the Franciscans had survived—Fray Antonio Bordoy, who was at the mission itself, and Fray Francisco Casañas. The labors of the Fathers at San Francisco de los Texas, while not without a certain amount of success, were discouraging; and on August 21, 1693, the viceroyal government ordered Father Massanet and the friars who remained with him at the mission to abandon their post. In October, 1693, after burying the bells, they set out with sad hearts for Querétaro. "With his departure from Texas," writes Engelhardt, "Massanet disappears from history."[10]

2. Santísimo Nombre de Maria (1690).

Before a year had passed after the establishment of the Mission of San Francisco, Father Miguel Fontcubierta had died during an epidemic of fever (February 5, 1691), in which almost three thousand of the Texas Indians who were under his care were wiped out in a single month. Father Francisco Casañas decided to leave and found a mission in a healthier location.

---

[9] Engelhardt, *Missionary Labors etc.*, (Franciscan Herald) March, 1915, p. 108.
[10] *Ibid.*, May, 1915, p. 187.

This he did in October, 1690, locating among the Neches Indians in what is now the southwestern part of Cherokee county.[11] In his report, presented to the Viceroy a year later, Casañas claims that in spite of almost insuperable obstacles to his success among the Neches, the mission would prove a permanent outpost of the Spanish government; but de Galve included Santísimo Nombre de María in his decree of abandonment, and in October, 1693, the mission was deserted. In fact, while Casañas was in Mexico City for the purpose of giving his report to the government, Santísimo Nombre de María was destroyed by a flood, and all the Spaniards took refuge at the Mission San Francisco de los Texas across the Neches River. Father Casñas was sent (1693) to one of the New Mexican missions and was martyred there three years later, thus winning for himself the glory of being the proto-martyr of the Querétaran Fathers.

Governor Terán apparently had lost all interest in the two missions. He believed that his work was finished when the result of the expedition of 1690-91 had proved the falsity of the report that the French adventurers had founded a settlement within Spanish territory. His policy was further guided by his decision that not until Spanish presidios had been set up in the chief Indian towns, could the missionaries expect to make any headway in converting the Indians of east Texas.

Dunn writes: "After the return of Governor Terán to Mexico, interest in Texas seems to have perceptibly waned. No effort was made to revive the plans that had been formulated. Not until the latter part of the year did the vice-regal government manifest sufficient interest in Texas to inquire as to the progress that was being made by missionaries there. . . . At this time the province of Texas was abandoned after four years of fruitless effort and expense. The interest of the vice-regal government in that region had first been aroused by the intrusions of the French. The movement for the founding of missions, begun when the foreign menace seemed past, grew in scope when rumors of French activity were received. These larger plans were necessarily relinquished, however, when the intractable nature of the Indians was fully realized. The first occupation of Texas was an enterprise conceived and executed by the colonial officials of

---

[11] Bolton, "Native Tribes About the East Texas Missions," in the Texas State Historical Association *Quarterly,* April, 1908, pp. 206–208.

New Spain. The home government, with its energies absorbed in war, had little share in it, save to approve measures after they had already been adopted. While ready to sanction a movement to extend the Catholic religion and the domain of the king, it showed little direct and active interest in the Texas project. This comparative indifference was perhaps chiefly due to the opinion prevalent among royal officials in Spain that the Gulf region, especially that portion west of the Mississippi River, offered little inducement for colonization to a foreign nation, and that it was needless to expend large sums for its development and defense."[12]

3. *San Francisco de los Neches, Purísima Concepción, San José (1716).*

"The question may well be asked," writes a recent scholar in the field of Texas history, "whether these several and unsuccessful efforts to establish missions among the Tejas and Cadadachos were of any permanent value in the evolution of Texas. Without doubt, they were. A certain amount of substance and energy must always be wasted in forcing civilization into an unbroken wilderness. Each new country has its peculiar difficulties, only experience can teach how to overcome. Paths must be traced, mountains and valleys traversed, boundaries searched out, and coasts and rivers explored; and these things are seldom accomplished without the lavish expediture of men and means. That remote inland settlements are difficult to establish and more difficult to maintain; that the organization of an extensive mission system must be the slow work of years, and not the accomplishment of a summer campaign; that the conversion of even the most tractable of Indians must be a mingling of force with persuasion; and, finally, that the mission could thrive only when it existed side by side with the presidio (garrison),—these were the useful deductions from Fray Damian Massanet's costly experimenting.

"And there were other lessons of value. A more correct idea of the geography of Texas was obtained; the most important rivers were named and their courses determined; roads were marked out from Coahuila to the plains of southwest Texas along

[12] *Op. cit.,* pp. 138–139, 144–145.

which Spanish civilization could advance more surely; and the Bay of Espíritu Santo became an easy and familiar landing place for later expeditions. All these facts were worth something when the time came at length to undertake seriously the task of opening the lands beyond the Rio Grande settlement. The little log church of San Francisco and its companion mission by the Neches, although ephemeral and productive of no immediate good, in the larger outlook were eminently worthwhile; for they served as an admonition and a warning when, twenty years later, the friars came again to stretch their line of larger and more substantial churches from the Rio Grande to the Sabine."[13]

Almost twenty-five years passed, however, before any further effort to establish missions among the Texas Indians was made. A second mission under the patronage of their saintly Founder was begun in 1716 by the Franciscans near the Neches River and was named San Francisco de los Neches. This was on the opposite bank of the river from the earlier Mission San Francisco. By the aid of diaries and archaeological observations, Bolton has established the location of this Querétaran mission among the Neches in the region of Mound Prairie about five miles southwest of Alto in Cherokee County. The Franciscans who established the mission were Father Francisco Hidalgo, who had retired from Texas twenty-two years before, Father Gabriel Vergara, Father Benito Sánchez, Father Manuel Castellanos, and Father Pedro Pérez de Mesqúia. They set out from Saltillo on January 21, 1716, and at San Juan Bautista, south of the Rio Grande, they were met by a group of Zacatecan Fathers who were on their way to Texas. The end of their journey was reached on July 3, 1717, and the mission of San Francisco de los Neches was established.

Two other missions were founded by this same group of Franciscans—the Mission of Purísima Concepción, which was begun on July 7, 1717, and a few days later, the Mission of San José among the Nazones, ten leagues north of Purísima Concepción. Father Espinosa, who was in charge of the San Francisco Mission wrote a complete history of these establishments in his *Chrónica Apostólica.*

These three missions had only a short independent existence,

---

[13] R. C. Clark, "Beginnings of Texas" in the Texas State Historical Association *Quarterly*, January, 1902, p. 193.

The Querétaran Missions—I: (1690-1731)   31

when they were transferred to San Antonio in 1730. In 1727, Pedro de Rivera was sent to these missions to inspect the general conditions of the work, and the guardian, Father Gabriel de Vergara, advised him to recommend to the government the concentration of the Indians into reservations. De Rivera, on his return, advised the suppression of Purísima Concepción on the Angelina River, and in spite of the protest of Father Miguel Servillano de Parédes, the head of the Querétaran college, the three missions were transferred to the vicinity of the San Antonio River, where as Espinosa has written, "it would be easier to collect (the Indians) and induce them to devote themselves to agriculture and community life under the shadow of the Cross."[14]

Engelhardt tells us that the Fathers were most reluctant to abandon their work in the interior of Texas, even though apparently the ten years spent among the Indians had not resulted in much success. They were encouraged, however, by the fact that their new field lay in the midst of three tribes who had not yet heard the message of the Gospel. The same names were kept with the new missions, with the exception of San José which was changed to San Juan Capistrano.

The isolated situation of these three missions was a matter of grave concern to the civil authorities and after this decision to erect a presidio and a town at the Rio San Antonio, the viceroy gave orders for the establishment of new missions between the San Antonio district and the Rio Guadalupe. In this way came about the fourth Querétaran mission.

4. *San Antonio de Valero (1718)*.

This mission, named in honor of the Viceroy, owes its existence to Father Antonio de San Buenaventura y Olivares. He is numbered among that zealous band of Franciscans of the College of Holy Cross, so graphically described by his fellow Querétaran, Espinosa. He had a very keen interest in Texas. In 1709 that interest led him across the Rio Grande River and he journeyed as far as the Rio Frio, in company with Father Espinosa.

With the permission (May, 1718) of the Viceroy, Marqués de Valero, Father Olivares transferred his Xarame Indian Mis-

---

[14] *Chrónica Apostólica y Seráfica de todos los Colegios de Esta Nueva-España* (Mexico, 1746), p. 415.

sion of San Francisco de Solano from the southern banks of the Rio Grande to the Rio San Antonio de Padua in Texas. Father Olivares maintained himself for more than a year on the site chosen. He may, therefore, properly and justly be regarded as the founder of Mission San Antonio de Valero on the Rio San Antonio de Padua. In the beginning Father Olivares was alone. The friar assigned to the mission had died before leaving the Rio Grande. While laboring among the neighboring savages, especially the Payays, who spoke the Xarame language, Father Olivares broke his leg, and a messenger was quickly sent to the Rio Grande mission to notify the Fathers. It is said that Father Pedro Muñoz came the distance of eighty leagues in forty consecutive hours. After receiving the consolation of the sacraments at the hand of Father Muñoz, efforts were made to remedy the fracture. No surgeon was available and a soldier undertook to set the leg. Then by means of some household remedies, the missionary was restored, but not until he had spent a long time in bed, which must have been a sore affliction for such an energetic priest.[15] Soon after his recovery, Father Olivares moved his mission to the other bank, doubtless to the site it still occupies under the name of the Alamo, famous for the massacre of 1836, at the hands of Santa Anna.[16]

The name San Antonio de Padua had been given to this part of Texas as early as 1691, when Terán's expedition stopped at the present site of the city on June 13, 1691, and a military Mass was celebrated.

It was not long before the success of the mission at San Antonio became known to the priests in eastern Texas. Father Olivares had a visit from Father Espinosa, Superior of the Querétaran missions in the region of the Neches River, when on his way to Mexico City to report the unhappy outlook at his post. At San Antonio, Espinosa met Governor Alarcón, who had come with supplies for the eastern missions. Father Espinosa decided to entrust the written reports to the care of a companion, Father Matias Sans de San Antonio, a Zacatecan friar, while he himself would act as a guide to Alarcón on his way to the Texas missions. Father Matias went on to the Viceroy.

By this time San Antonio had become a half-way point for

---
[15] *Chrónica Apostólica y Seráfica etc.*, p. 450.
[16] Cf. Dunn, *op. cit.*, p. 191.

communication with the vice-regal headquarters. This took place before December, 1718, the time of Alarcón's departure for the return to Mexico. In 1719 San Antonio became a place of refuge for the missionaries among the eastern tribes of Texas, when they were threatened and actually assaulted by the French who had come from Louisiana. Both the Querétaran and the Zacatecan friars made their way to San Antonio in the summer of 1719. Father Espinosa and Father Margil, the superiors of these respective missions, were the last to leave the eastern missions for San Antonio. Father Espinosa did not remain long as he wanted to make a report in person to the Viceroy. Father Margil and the other Franciscans built thatched quarters for themselves at San Antonio and remained there until 1721. In April, 1721, the result of Father Espinosa's visit to the Viceroy was very forcibly seen at San Antonio. The governor of Coahuila, Marqués de San Miguel de Aguayo, with an expeditionary force of about five hundred men, set out for the missions and was joyously received by the refugees at San Antonio.

In 1731 Mission San Antonio de Valero came to be the headquarters for Father Santa Ana, President of the Querétaran missions of Texas. He came to San Antonio de Valero in 1731 and exercised his official duties from this mission for three years, then he transferred his office to Mission Concepción. Between 1731 and 1745 Christian influence went out to more than forty tribes who lived in the regions of the middle Colorado and the Rio Grande, the Gulf Coast and the San Antonio Road. The baptismal records of San Antonio de Valero bear testimony to the wide range of its influence among the Indians.[17] During the first decade of its existence there had been two hundred and fifty baptisms, and by 1740 this number had increased to eight hundred and thirty-seven.

In the official report of 1762 of all the Texas missions, required by Father Manuel de Náxera, San Antonio de Valero showed to good advantage. A church of "harmonious architecture" was being built of quarried stone. A convent of two stories in height and fifty *varas* in length and breadth with two patios and arched cloisters served as an abode for the Querétarans. Its work shop was busy with four looms and fabrics of cotton and wool were being made from the material stored in

---

[17] Cf. Bolton, *Texas in the Middle Eighteenth Century*, p. 16.

two rooms. The pueblo about the mission consisted of seven rows of houses, all of stone, with arched porticoes, doors, and windows. Through the plaza ran a stream of water, with willows and fruit trees on its banks. Its fields were tilled, fenced in, and watered by irrigation ditches. Maize, chile beans, and cotton were produced in abundance on the farm lands of the mission. Cattle, sheep, and goats grazed on its pastures. In the number of stock this mission ranked third of the Querétaran missions, San Francisco and San Juan surpassing. But in the spiritual work, the increase in baptisms at San Antonio was about equal to the combined efforts of the other three missions. More than forty-four hundred Indians had been baptized in all the missions, since the beginning, but half of these baptisms were administered in the seventeen years preceding 1762. In the important work of inducing the Indians to live a community life, the Fathers at San Antonio de Valero had two hundred and seventy-five Indians in its pueblo, this being a few more than those of the other three missions. This mission was also distinguished by some of the Fathers in its personnel.

About 1750 Father Francisco Mariano de los Dolores y Viana succeeded Father Benito Fernandez de Santa Ana as President of the Querétaran missions. He made San Antonio de Valero his headquarters. He spent almost thirty years as a missionary in Texas, coming to that field about 1733. Until 1763 he made his energy, courage, and zeal felt in a manner that makes the knowledge of his life indispensable for the story of the Franciscans in Texas. His project of the present San Gabriel River, in Milam County, reveals him as a man of no mean ability. San Antonio de Valero numbered men of literary attainments in its list of missionaries. One of these was Father Diego Martín García, who copied in his own handwriting some of the older records, and in 1745 he wrote his *Breve y Legal Noticia* which is one of the main sources for information on missionary methods. Another of the Fathers at San Antonio de Valero who has since become famous in historiography is Juan Domingo Arricivita. After returning to Querétaro he wrote, in 1792, his chronicles of Holy Cross College, one of the greatest contributions to the history of Texas.[18]

These workers at Valero gave more than their intellectual

---

[18] Cf. *ibid.,* p. 96.

The Querétaran Missions—I: (1690-1731)

talents—Alonso Geraldo de Terreros, assigned to San Antonio de Valero in 1748, gave his life. He died at the hands of the Comanches in the San Sabá missionary district in March, 1758, just ten years after his assignment to San Antonio de Valero.[19] The extent of Querétaran activity from 1690 to 1763 was practically confined by that latter date to the missions in and around the present City of San Antonio.

Within the vicinity of San Antonio de Valero, the Querétarans erected in 1731 three other missions: San Francisco de la Espada to the south; San Juan Capistrano to the east; and Concepción, which had been transferred from East Texas. The geographical salient, therefore, of Querétaran activity in west central Texas was not a large one, since practically all the labors of the missionaries belonging to the college of the Holy Cross were confined in and around the present city of San Antonio. Meanwhile, contact was growing with the Indians of central Texas and within the next generation, a busy mission center was to be erected along the San Xavier River (San Gabriel).

---

[19] Palóu's *Life of Junípero Serra,* translated by C. Scott Williams and edited by George Wharton James, pp. 39-40, Pasadena, 1913.

CHAPTER IV.

The Querétaran Missions—II: (1731–1763).

During the next fifteen years (1731-1746), no further mission sites were established by the Querétaranos. These years coincided with a growing conviction on the part of the Spanish officials that central Texas should be explored and settled, in order to increase its value as part of the great buffer Texas was destined to be against French encroachment from Louisiana.

Up to the publication of Bolton's *Texas in the Middle Eighteenth Century* in 1915, the period from 1721 to 1746 was considered scant of importance, both in the civil and ecclesiastical history of the province. The creation of the Province of Nuevo Santander, north of the Province of Nuevo León, and east of the Province of Coahuila, in 1746, brought central Texas into compact political organization under the Viceroy and from that time until the acquisition of Louisiana by Spain during the same century, exploration and settlement in this part of Texas was carried out in increasing rapidity. Bolton calls the period from 1731 to 1745, "one of testing the original establishments, rather than founding new ones."[1]

After 1745, when the missions on the San Gabriel River in central Texas were begun, they were to form as San Antonio did farther west the center and defense of Spanish occupation towards the east. Politically speaking, Bolton has named the period from 1731 to 1745: *The Province on Trial.* "The most conspicuous work of the period," he writes, "was done by the missionaries. No new missions were founded in the interval, but the missionaries in charge of the missions already established instructed their neophytes with commendable zeal, improved the material plants of their missions, and sought new recruits among many new bands constantly more removed from the mission centers. During the fifteen years a score or more priests, not to mention the lay brothers, labored at the San Antonio missions alone. The central figure among them was Fray Benito

---
[1] *Texas in the Middle Eighteenth Century*, p. 14.

The Querétaran Missions—II: (1731-1763)

Ferandez de Santa Ana, who arrived in 1731 and most of the time thereafter until 1750 was president of the four Querétaran missions. After living three years at San Antonio de Valero, he made his headquarters at Concepción. Scarcely less conspicuous was Father Francisco Mariano de los Dolores y Viana, who arrived in 1733 and remained until 1763, succeeding Father Santa Ana as president. His residence was at Mission San Antonio de Valero. Among the missionaries of this period were two who later became martyrs. These were Fathers José Ganzábal and Alonzo Giraldo de Terreros, the first of whom was killed on the San Gabriel River in 1752, the other on the San Sabá in 1758. None did a more valuable service for history than diligent Fray Martín García, of mission San Antonio, who wrote a long disquisition concerning the management of Indians, and copied in his own handwriting many of the older records of the missions to preserve them from destruction. The painstaking reports and correspondence of the missionaries as a whole will always stand as a monument to their training and intelligence, and though as yet little known, will constitute a priceless treasury of history and ethnology.

"Notable among the efforts with the outlying bands were those of Father Mariano de los Dolores, who after 1733 made frequent visits to the Tonkawan tribes near the middle Brazos River. In 1739 a general epidemic swept through the missions at San Antonio, after which there was renewed activity among the distant tribes. In the year named, the Tacame, after having deserted Mission San Francisco, were taken to that of San Antonio de Valero. About 1745 Father Juan Mariano de Molina visited the Cujane, Karankawa, Manos de Perro, and Piguique, tribes living in the main down the coast to the southwest of the Guadalupe River. In the year last named the missionaries of San Juan Bautista and San Bernardo prepared an expedition to the natives of the lower Rio Grande, but it was prevented by a revolt at Lampazos in which the coast tribes joined.

"The foregoing are only a few of the recorded missionary expeditions made during the period. Besides these there must have been numerous other journeys equally notable. This is clearly shown by the data contained in the mission records. At mission San Antonio de Valero alone no less than forty bands of tribes were represented by the baptisms between 1731 and

1745. In general they included people living between the middle Colorado and the Rio Grande, the San Antonio Road and the Gulf Coast. The original tribes at the mission of Concepción were three—the Pajalat, Siquipil, and Tilpacopal—but by 1745 members of at least fifteen others had been attracted thither. The tribes taken to the three new missions—that is those transferred to San Antonio in 1731—during this period were mainly from the coastwise district rather than from the interior."[2]

5. *Nuestra Señora de los Dolores del Rio de San Xavier (1746).*

Owing to the solid progress of the Missions in and around San Antonio during these years, it was natural that the work of the missionaries would be made known by these Indians to other tribes lying between the western and eastern part of the province.

Fray Mariano de los Dolores y Viana, a Querétaran stationed at San Antonio de Valero, after 1735, had made some tentative excursions into central Texas and had visited four of the principal tribes living there. In 1745, four chiefs of the tribes in question with some followers came to San Antonio and begged the Fathers to come among them to found a mission. Efforts were made to have the tribes come permanently to San Antonio, but this failing, the commissary visitor, Fray Francisco Xavier Ortiz, gave the necessary permission, and in 1746, Fray Mariano started for the settlements of these tribes and chose a mission site on San Xavier River (now the San Gabriel), at what is now Brushy Creek,[3] giving it the name: La Mision Nuestra Señora de los Dolores del Rio de San Xavier, which became known generally as the Mission San Francisco Xavier. In founding this mission Father Mariano was assisted by Fray Benito Fernández de Santa Ana, then president of the Querétaran missions.

Before a year had passed, Fray Mariano had spent five thousand dollars, a large sum in those days, for the equipment of the mission. "Practically all that we know of active operation (at San Xavier)," writes Bolton, "between June, 1746, and February, 1748, is that the missionaries were there, from time to time at least, planting crops, catechising the Indians, and holding them

---

[2] *Ibid.,* p. 16.
[3] Bolton has located the Mission nine miles to the north of Rockdale (*ibid.,* p. 225, 230).

until the project should be definitely supported and something permanent undertaken."[4]

Here again, as in the case of San Antonio de Valero, other missions were founded in the vicinity of San Xavier.

6. San Ildefonso (1749).

There were grave objections by some of the Spanish officials to the founding of the San Xavier missions and to its complete development; but on December 23, 1747, the Viceroy gave his consent to the establishment of the other missions on the San Xavier River. This came as the result of many petitions made by Fray Mariano and the Querétarans, and when the royal consent reached Mexico in the following summer by a *cedula* issued on April 16, 1748, all difficulties were removed and the work went ahead.

Fray Mariano fell sick about this time, indeed, he was incapacitated for more than a year after April, 1748, and Fray Santa Ana supervised the labors of the Fathers and the Indians at the Mission San Xavier. The success of the work is evident in a report sent by Santa Ana on March 10, 1749: "The mission of San Xavier, having some established form, has been situated on this river since February of last year. Not counting those who have died Christians, there are listed in it of the nation of the Mayeye thirty-two men, and among them only two old men, one of sixty and the other of eighty years of age. The women number only forty-one, because this nation has been attacked by the Apaches. The youths, maidens, and children, likewise number only thirteen, for the same reason. Of the nation of the Hierbipiamos (*sic*) there are thirty-one men, there not being any old men among them; women, twenty-one, boys and girls, eleven. This nation suffered the same assaults as the former. Of the nation of the Yojuanes twenty-six men, none of them old; women, twenty-three; boys and girls, seven; youths, twenty-eight. With these three nations there are some Tanchagues who struggle with the Apaches, whom they attacked last year before the governor of Coahuila did so."[5]

---

[4] *Ibid.*, p. 161.
[5] Cited *ibid.*, p. 190; Cf. Dunn, "Apache Relations in Texas," in the Texas State Historical Association *Quarterly* (XIV, 254).

San Ildefonso, the second of these missions in central Texas, was erected between December 27, 1748, and February 25, 1749, under the supervision of Father Santa Ana. The third mission was erected shortly afterwards.

7. Nuestra Señora de la Candelaria (1749).

In spite of serious obstacles, such as the desertion of some of the Indians and, what was far more serious, the hostility of Governor Barrio to the missionaries, Santa Ana founded the third mission for which the viceroy had given permission, not far from the San Xavier itself. The Candelaria was reserved for the Coco and other Karankawan tribes who dwelt between San Xavier and the Gulf coast, many of whom were being cared for by the Zacatecan fathers, who had erected missions in that section.

For a while these three missions on the San Gabriel River made excellent progress. They were visited in May, 1749, by Governor Barrio, whose report of that month to the viceroy relates that he found in the San Xavier missions, fifty men, thirty-three women, and twenty-seven children. In Mission Candelaria, there were twenty-five men, twenty-five women, and twenty-two children. At Mission San Ildefonso, he counted forty-six men, forty-eight women, and thirty-one children. The total for the three missions was 322 persons.

Fray Mariano gives us at this time a few details of the life of the Indians: "In all the Missions the Indians say prayers morning and afternoon. They live congregated in pueblos, and labor in so far as their willingness permits, making their fences and clearing their corn patches. In Texas (i.e. eastern Texas) they are not congregated, much less do they say prayers. At the same time, they are in the missions without your Lordship having ordered them called, the soldiers bringing them. Therefore, it is because they desire it. It is thus manifest that these missions are a fact, and that the Indians do not live like the Texas do to the present."[6]

The immediate cause for the decline and actual abandonment of the San Xavier missions came about through a dispute between Captain Felipe de Rábago y Terán, who was sent by the

---

[6] Cited by Bolton *ibid.*, p. 201.

Viceroy Revilla Gigeod in May, 1751, to establish a presidio at the San Xavier, and the Franciscans.

Arricivita thus describes the events: "As soon as the captain arrived he showed that the conditions at the presidio and in the country were not according to his ideas. The solitude to him was frightful. The cottonwood along the river appeared a poor substitute for the promenade to which he had been accustomed, and the chirping of the cricket and the beetle a most disagreeable orchestra. In the end, the country seemed to him more insufferable than Siberia. To this state of mind the fact contributed much that he possessed no more education for administering justice than what he had picked up in drawing up accounts and warrants. The result was that in all the cases brought before him the captain's only associate judge was irascibility. From it emanated all his decisions, which he would execute in fury, inconsiderately, and without taking time to think. The very first case was the cruel imprisonment of an unfortunate married man whom the captain amid derision and much unnecessary noise had arrested on the road fronting San Antonio. On Christmas night the prisoner seized the opportunity and fled to Mission Candelaria, where he took refuge in the church. Rábago's fury, however, would not let him stop to think of the consequences of violating the right of sanctuary. Nor did the solemnity of the great feast of the Nativity restrain the haughty officer. Mounting his horse in a rage he galloped to the Mission, burst into the church while holy Mass was being celebrated, and sacreligiously dragged the poor refugee out, despite the supplications and protests of the missionary."[7]

Further tortures of the poor victim aroused the Franciscans and Rábago was excommunicated. He had, moreover, without consulting the Fathers recommended an amalgamation of the three missions at a new site near the presidio of San Marcos. To bring about peace, Father Mariano was ordered to be removed, and was succeeded by Father Alonso Girarldo de Terrerros, but the enmity between Rábago and the friars was still alive. In May 1752 Father Ganzábal was murdered at Mission Candelaria, and all but one of the Fathers of the three missions fled to San Antonio in fear of their lives.

---

[7] *Crónica Seráfica y Apostólica del Colegio De Propaganda Fide de la Santa Cruz de Querétaro*, pp. 330–331. Mexico, 1792.

After the murder of Ganzábal, the Indians began to desert the missions. Rábago was superseded by his brother, Don Pedro Rábago in August, 1754. The new captain "urged the abandonment of the whole San Xavier undertaking, and by this time the missionaries, with whom the new commander was popular, were ready to agree. The few neophytes, Rábago thought, might be taken to the missions at San Antonio, and the soldiers and missionaries transferred to the Apache country, on the San Sabá or the Florida (Concho) River, which he had explored in 1748. Because of bad season the site at San Xavier had proved unhealthful, and to this drawback were added tales of horrible manifestations of nature. In consequence, after several unavailing appeals for permission to move, in the summer of 1755 the soldiers, missionaries and a few neophytes, with their belongings, but without permission, to the springs of the San Marcos River, bent their way. Thus ended ten years' effort to establish and maintain missions on the San Xavier River, in the country of the Tonkawa."[8]

8. Nuestra Señora de Guadalupe (1759).

Fray Mariano had no intention of neglecting the neophytes of the three abandoned San Xavier missions. In fact, Arricivita says that he went back from time to time to visit his charges. In June, 1756, Mariano suggested to Father Ortiz the establishment of a mission on the Guadalupe River and proposed the site of what is now New Braunfels, as best suited to the purpose. Captain Diego Ramón of the San Marcos garrison promised aid for the new foundation. The mission was established during the following year (1757) but was abandoned in 1758 after the destruction of the San Sabá Mission, since it had not a sufficient garrison to protect it from the marauding Indians, then on the warpath.

The definite time of abandonment by the Querétarans of their Texas Missions can not be accurately given. Shea says that "soon after the year 1763 the college of Querétaro withdrew from Texas, leaving that field to the Colleges of Zacatecas and Guadalajara."[9] After the suppression of the Jesuits in Mexico

---
[8] Bolton, *op. cit.*, p. 56.
[9] *History of the Catholic Church in the United States*, Vol. I, p. 509. Shea's authority is Arricivita, *op. cit.*, p. 437.

in 1767, some of their colleges were turned over to the Franciscans. Owing to this added labor, the Querétarans handed over the government of their Texas establishment to the Fathers of the Zacatecan College.

Such was the tragic end of the missions, for the establishment of which the Queréterans had spared no effort to make them permanent. Eight missions may not seem to be a noteworthy record for a period of some sixty years; but it is only by comparing the difficult conditions prevailing in Texas during the period under review (1690-1763) with all the means of communication we have today, that we may reach a just estimate of the zeal of the Franciscans in converting the Indians of Texas and in bringing to them the benefits of civilization.[10]

We now turn to the work of a second apostolic college, that of Zacatecas, and to the missions erected by the Fathers who belonged to it.

---

[10] A partial list of the missionary priests at San Antonio is given in E. J. P. Schmitt, *A List of Franciscan Missionaries in Texas, 1528-1859* (Austin, 1901). It contains some evident errors in transcribing and confuses Spanish and English forms. Those named for the years 1731-1745 are the following: Alonso Giraldo de Terreros, Benito Fernández de Santa Ana, Juan Hurtado de Jesús María, Ignacio Antonio Cyprian, Joseph Gonzales, Salud de Amaya, Gabriel de Vergara, Francisco Joseph de Frias, Henrique Arquellos (sic de la Concepción), Phelipe Miguel Suarez Espinosa, Joseph Hurtado de Jesús María, Joseph Guadalupe Prado, Joachim Camargo de Santa Ana, Diego Martín García, Lud. (elsewhere Juan) Maria and de Molina, Joseph Francisco de Gonzábal, Juan de los Angeles. The San Antonio mission which thus became a sort of refuge for the central and eastern Texas missions is described by Fray Fernández de Santa Ana, *Descripción de las Missiones del Colegio de la Santa Cruz en el Rio de San Antonio, Año de 1740*, MS. in *Memorias de Nueva España* (XXVIII, 200-207).

CHAPTER V.

The Zacatecan Missions (1716-1793).

Second in importance to the College of the Holy Cross of Querétaro in the history of Franciscan missionary efforts in Texas is the Colegio de Propaganda Fide of Guadalupe (Nuestra Señora de Guadalupe) erected in the city of Zacatecas in 1706. The Zacatecans, as the Fathers of that college were known, began their missionary work in Texas in 1716, when they inaugurated the foundations of missions in eastern Texas. The archives of the college of Guadalupe contain an interesting series of documents for the history of the Texas missions. The Zacatecans assumed more important work when the Querétaran missions of San Antonio were turned over to their charge, and so remained until the days of secularization after the end of the Spanish régime.

The glory of the Zacatecan friars is the Venerable Fray Antonio Margil, who was President of the Zacatecan missions when they began their labors in eastern Texas.

Antonio Margil was born at Valencia, Spain, on August 18, 1657. He entered the Franciscan Order in his native city in 1673, and after completing his theological training, volunteered for the Indian missions of New Spain, where he arrived in the summer of 1683. For the next twenty-three years he was a member of the Querétaran community in the College of the Holy Cross.

From the pages of Arricivita's *Crónica Seráfica,* which remains today a basic source for the history of the Texas missions, John Gilmary Shea has drawn the chief factors of Margil's life. "Though young," he writes, "he was at once associated with older and experienced fathers in giving missions at Querétaro and Mexico, edifying all by his zeal and mortification. Having been selected to labor in Yucatan, he journeyed on foot to Vera Cruz, where he embarked, and reaching his destination, began with Father Melchior of Jesus, his mission life among the Indians, till the two apostles sank under the labors and mortifications near Chiapa, and received Extreme Unction. Recovering by what seemed a miracle, they traversed Central America, giving constant missions in what are now the Republics of that part of the Continent. He converted the Talamanacas, Terrebas, and other tribes, and was preparing to confirm his labors by establishing solid missions, when he and his associates were summoned back to the college. The two Franciscans, full of obedience at once set out, resigning the Indian missions into the hands of the Bishop of Nicaragua. Their superior, learning the important work on which they were engaged, revoked his order, and the Bishop of Nicaragua assigned to them the district of Vera Paz, where they labored among the Cooles and Lacandones, though their lives were in constant danger. Such was the ability of Father Margil in acquiring languages, in comprehending the pagan ideas and refuting them, in giving solid instruction, and in guiding neophytes in the path of Christian life, that bishops placed bodies of missionaries even of other orders under his direction, though the humble religious endeavored in vain to avoid such a position. He crowned his labors by establishing a Missionary College de Propaganda Fide in the city of Guatemala, of which he was elected Guardian. His labors and his knowledge seemed supernatural; in many cases he appeared to be laboring in two places at once, and the secret idolatries of the Indians which escaped the knowledge of others he exposed and suppressed."[1]

Margil's was the chief influence which brought about the foundation of the second Franciscan apostolic college at Zacatecas, and he was appointed its guardian on June 25, 1706. Ten years later he began the Zacatecan foundations in eastern Texas. In 1722 he returned to Zacatecas, and on August 16, 1726, died at the Convento Grande de San Francisco, in Mexico City. His life had been so extraordinarily devoted to penance, mortification and prayer, that the Franciscans shortly after his death, began the cause for his beatification. A century later (1836) Pope Gregory XVI proclaimed his virtues heroic and he thereby

---

[1] *Op. cit.,* I, 489; Espinosa, *El Peregrino Septentrionale Atlante,* Mexico, 1737; Valencia, 1742; *Nuevas Empressas, Mexico,* 1747; Villaplana, *Vida Portentosa del Americano Septentrional Apostol, El V.P.F. Ano. Margil,* Madrid, 1775; Guzmán, *Notizie della Vita del Ven Servo di Dio Fr. Antonio Margil de Jesús,* Rome, 1836; Arricivita, *Crónica Seráfica y Apostólica,* Mexico, 1792, ii, pp. 1–98.

bears the title of Venerable—one of the few in the New World to whom this honor has been given.

In the Apostolic brief of Gregory XVI we read:

> The Venerable Antonio Margil, professed priest of the Friars Minor Observant of St. Francis, completely fulfilled the command of the Divine Master, when He told His Disciples, 'Go into all the world, preach the Gospel and teach all nations.' For no sooner had he ended his novitiate than he occupied himself wholly in spreading the Word of God. Being soon called to the Missions in the Indies, he gladly received the Apostolic Ministry and leaving his country, crossed the ocean. In the New World he was not content to labor only in known regions, but penetrating to the furthest and most inaccessible parts, he visited unfriendly nations, savage tribes, speaking unknown tongues, barbarous in their cruelty, overwhelmed in the darkness of ignorance, given over to witchcraft and superstitions, idolaters, everywhere preaching Christ, the true God, and travailing to teach them the commands of the Gospel and a more civilized manner of life. Trusting in God, the Venerable Antonio daily undertook the most arduous journeys, without scrip or purse or shoes; patiently suffering hunger and thirst and all manner of hardships; fearlessly enduring insults, bonds, arrows, the stake, ofttimes the danger of death, and thirsting after martyrdom, if only he might drag these wretched souls from the clutches of the devil and make them subject to Christ. Strengthened by the help of heaven, he brought many thousands of men; aforetime living like wild beasts, to religion and baptized them; destroyed the worship of false gods, did away with superstitions, broke up idols, and built Chapels, Mission Houses and Colleges for the Propagation of the Faith in the remotest regions.[2]

1. *Nuestra Señora de Guadalupe (1716)*.

This first Zacatecan mission was dedicated to Mexico's patron saint—Our Lady of Guadalupe. The mission once stood at what is now the center of the present town of Nacogdoches. Espinosa, who accompanied Father Margil, has described the adverse conditions against which the members of the first mission had to

---

[2] Cited by Kirwin, *History of the Diocese of Galveston*, pp. 20–21 (Galveston, 1922). The history of the Zacatecan Missions will be found in Sotomayor, *Historia del Apostólica Colegio de Nuestra Señora de Guadalupe de Zacatecas*, 2 vols. (Zacatecas, 1889).

The Zacatecan Missions (1716–1793)   47

contend. "For two years," Espinosa writes, "the want and hardships which the Fathers endured in the missions of Texas were keenly felt; but it seems they were unavoidable. From the time the missionaries entered that country, in 1716, no aid whatever reached them, and as the supplies which they brought along were very few, they soon gave out and we were reduced to great straits.

"During the years 1717 and 1718, owing to the severity of the drought, the harvest of corn and beans among the Indians was very poor. As we usually received some provisions from the natives, it was inevitable that when they themselves suffered want, we should also feel the pangs of hunger. Although we had written of our distress to the Colleges of Santa Cruz and Gaudalupe, and although they had taken energetic steps to relieve our necessities by appealing to the Viceroy, His Excellency, the Marqués de Valero, and the Royal Junta or council could do no more than direct a governor to proceed at once with soldiers and provisions to Coahuila and Texas.

"I do not intend that through my reports the reputation of any officer be blackened, but it is certain that, in the year 1717, at the request of Fr. Superior of the Rio Grande Missions, a corporal and fifteen soldiers, accompanied by some friars, were despatched to Texas in order to transport the supplies which His Excellency, the Viceroy, had provided with an open hand. Nevertheless, these supplies which would have saved the whole province, remained forty leagues away in the desert like a ship run aground, because the soldiers who bore the provisions were impeded in their march by the swollen waters of the Trinity River, which had overflowed its banks for a distance of two leagues. The men waited until December, but as they noticed that the rains increased rather than diminished, and feared lest they themselves might perish, on a little oak-studded hill, and returned much discouraged to the Rio Grande del Norte. The friars, too, seeing that it was impossible to proceed, left a letter in the hand of some Texas Indians, who had remained in that region to plant their fields, and directed them to deliver it to us as soon as the River would permit passage. This letter told where the provisions had been hidden, and where the mail sent to us could be found. Of all this nothing was known to us until July, 1718.

"Before relating what then took place, I shall give a brief account of the miseries in which we found ourselves engulfed. In the first place, the daily bread, which in that country is Indian corn, was wanting. If, perchance, after running through the rancherias, a peck of corn was gathered, there was as much ado about it as if a great train of provisions had arrived. The scarcity of grain prevented us from making as much as a tortilla. When, by chance, we could get a mouthful of meat, we boiled a handful of corn and this answered the purpose of bread. Salt was entirely wanting, and thus, when we even had the good fortune to obtain beans, the lack of salt made them so unpalatable that they might have served as a cathartic. Meat in quantities was not to be had at all; and even if, on rare occasions, some compassionate Indian brought us a bit of venison, the want of salt rendered it little agreeable to the taste.

"Many a day dawned when there was absolutely nothing to eat at hand. Necessity, however, is the mother of invention. It occured to one of the Fathers that possibly the flesh of a crow might after all furnish us a meal. These birds were somewhat smaller than our crows, but they abounded in the trees, especially during the morning hours. By means of a gun surely we would be able to feast on meat every day. True, the color, flavor, and toughness of this meat were quite repugnant, but hunger made it so appetizing, that for the greater part of the year crow's meat formed one of our most delicious dishes. When the Fathers in the other missions heard of our discovery, they, too, provided their tables with crow's meat for the ordinary meals. On days of abstinence, however, our difficulties increased. As we had neither bread nor vegetables, we sought to appease our hunger by means of herbs, adding nuts by way of seasoning. On some days, the leaves of the mustard plant served as a most tasteful morsel, particularly when salty soil was found which rendered them more palatable.

"But the burden of distress was most heavily upon us not at the table but at the altar. Like all our other supplies, the wax gave out. Many days were spent in putting together the stubs and the drippings, until all the wax disappeared. After that we had recourse to candles made of fat; but even here the quantity we could collect among the Indians was so meager that even on days of obligation we were obliged to celebrate holy

Mass with but one tallow candle. The altar wine, too, became so scarce that only so much was put into the cruets as was absolutely necessary to make it lawful matter.

"In this extremity the Lord sent us some assistance through the venerable Fr. Antonio Margil, who was Superior of the Guadalupe missions, thirty leagues or more farther east. He paid us a visit, and we learnt that his mission suffered the same difficulties as our own, save that they possessed what was necessary for Holy Mass. As soon as the good Father had observed our lack of altar wine and wax, he jestingly confided to me that he, though an old man, had buried a bottle of wine to provide for the time of extreme necessity. When Father Margil, therefore, returned to his mission, he quickly sent us a quart bottle full of wine and a pound of wax. This we divided among us six priests, and thus, to our great consolation, we were enabled to celebrate Holy Mass again sometimes during the week and not only on Sundays and holydays of obligation, as heretofore. There were many other hardships which gave us opportunity of gaining merits during the two years, but these I leave to the imagination of the reader. I only hope that the sovereign Father of us all has found it worth while to mark down in his records what his servants endured, and that he will compensate them on the Last Day."[3]

Nuestra Señora de Guadalupe mission suffered the same disadvantages which had come to the eastern Texas missions of the Querétaran fathers, owing to the invasion of the territory by the French from Louisiana in 1719. The mission was closed for a while; but later, in August, 1721, the Marqués de Aguayo, Governor of the Province, re-established it at the same spot. Engelhardt is of the opinion that Father Margil sang the High Mass, at which Father Espinosa preached. This is characteristic of the friendly coöperation between the Querétarans and the Zacatecans, since Espinosa belonged to the former community. From this time until 1773, the Mission Guadalupe continued its labors among the Nacogdoches Indians. Owing to the hostility of the neighboring tribes, the Mission was abandoned in 1773. At the time of the Comanche uprising the inhabitants of Pilar de Bucareli took refuge at the former Guadalupe Mission in 1779. They were conducted thither by Captain

---

[3] *Chrónica Apostólica y Seráfica*, pp. 443–445 (Engelhardt's translation).

Gil Ybarbo and Father Garza, a Zacatecan friar. From this time on dates the modern town of Nacogdoches. "With the occupation of Nacogdoches," Bolton writes, "begins a new and important epoch in the history of the Texas-Louisiana frontier, and of the developments there Nacogdoches, instead of Adaes, became the chief center. The trading house asked for by Ybarbo was established and the Indian trade was reorganized. Nacogdoches, through being made headquarters for the trade and the distribution of presents among the dozen or more tribes in whose midst it lay, became the most important Indian agency in the province, while Ybarbo, as head of the community being among the Indians of the northeast the most influential Spaniard of the day. To Nacogdoches the government looked for the maintenance of influence among the Indians as a make-weight against the Anglo-Americans, who made their way to the borders of the country; and when, in 1803, the American frontier was carried across Louisiana to Texas, Nacogdoches became for a time equal if not superior in importance to Bexar, through being at once the outpost for aggressive movement by the Americans and for resistance by the Spaniards."[4]

2. *Nuestra Señora de los Dolores (1719).*

This second foundation was also made by the Venerable Fray Antonio de Margil. In a letter to Father Engelhardt, O.F.M. (June 26, 1915), Bolton identifies the spot where the Dolores Mission was erected in 1717, among the Ais Indians on the site of the present town of San Augustine, in San Augustine County, Texas.

Los Dolores Mission was also temporarily closed in 1719, at the time of the invasion by the French commandant of Natchitoches. It was restored at the time of the expedition of the Marqués de Aguayo.

In the same year (1717), the Zacatecans founded a third mission which does not properly belong to the history of Texas, that of San Miguel de los Adaes, in Louisiana, which was pillaged by the French in 1719, and restored by the Marqués de Aguayo.

For thirty years these three Zacatecan Missions had been zealously carrying on the work of evangelization among the

---
[4] *Texas in the Middle Eighteenth etc.,* pp. 445–446.

The Zacatecan Missions (1716-1793)

Nacogdoches, Ais, and Adaes Indians, but the results had not been encouraging. At the time of his inspection of the eastern Texas missions (1754), Father Juan De Dios Camberos reported to the viceroy that "notwithstanding the untiring efforts of the missionaries to reduce the Indians to mission life, it was notorious that they had succeeded in little more than the baptizing of a few children and fewer adults upon the death bed; and there was no hope that these tribes could ever be reduced to pueblos and induced to give up their tribal life. Under these circumstances four missionaries instead of five would suffice on that frontier. Since the Ais Indians consisted of only some forty families—perhaps two hundred persons—living within about fourteen leagues of Mission Nacogdoches, their mission could be suppressed, one friar going to Nacogdoches, to reside and from there ministering to the Ais, the other going to Bahía with the mission equipment, to work among the Karankawan tribes in question."[5]

When the order was given in June, 1754, to abandon the Ais Mission of Los Dolores, Father Vallejo, President of the Zacatecans, took the question up with the Spanish officials, and the order was reversed. In fact, so strongly did Father Vallejo describe the efforts made by the friars that permission was accorded to the Zacatecans in 1754, to found a mission among the Cujane Indians.

3. San José y San Miguel de Aguayo (1720)

The reported invasion of eastern Texas by the French from Natchitoches after the renewal of hostilities between Spain and France in 1719, caused the Viceroy Valero to send a relief expedition to that part of the province the next year. This expedition was placed in charge of the Governor de Aguayo. The personnel of the expedition gives us an insight into the fearful odds thrown against the labors of the missionaries by the Spanish officials, who perhaps in most cases acted unwittingly or without due regard to the consequences—one hundred men belonging to the band of five hundred men under Aguayo were of the lowest social and intellectual scale. This was, indeed, typical of many of the expeditions.

[5] *Ibid.*, p. 312.

Aguayo reached San Antonio in October, 1720, and while waiting for reinforcements, Father Margil obtained the permission to erect a Zacatecan Mission one or more leagues from San Antonio de Valero. The founding of the new mission, named in honor of the Governor, San José y San Miguel de Aguayo, occurred probably in March, 1720.

4. *Espíritu Santo de Zúñiga (1726-1749)*.

The first attempt to Christianize the Karankawas made by the Spanish Franciscans was the establishment of this mission in 1722. It was placed on the very site of Fort St. Louis founded by La Salle. The barbarous nature of the Karankawas led to the removal of the mission farther inland in 1726.

The ruins of this mission can be seen today near the present city of Victoria in Texas. This mission was moved in 1749 farther south to a better location on the San Antonio River. Many difficulties had arisen in the work of converting the Indians, and in 1753, the Fathers of Espíritu Santo decided to found a separate mission for the Karankawas. Father Camberos was sent to Mexico City to discuss the matter and in 1754 the viceroy gave the necessary permission. Father Vallejo, the President of the Texas Zacatecans, was not in favor of the projected mission, and in its place proposed a mission for the Cujanes.

5. *Nuestra Señora del Rosário de los Cujanes (1754)*.

The founder of the new mission, Father Camberos, had been in favor of abandoning the Los Dolores Mission at San Augustine, because he believed that the conversion of forty families was a poor showing after thirty years of effort on the part of the Zacatecan Fathers. He did not propose that these Ais Indians at Our Lady of Sorrows be abandoned but that they be entrusted to the care of the fathers at the Mission Guadalupe of Nacogdoches. He thought more than five hundred families of Cujane, Guapite, and Karankawa Indians in the territory near the town of modern Goliad were ready to be instructed in the mysteries of the Holy Faith. Father Camberos argued that it was a matter of duty to save the willing many "rather than to struggle hopelessly with the unwilling few." His suggestion took well with the viceroy and orders were issued to transfer the mission goods of Our Lady of Sorrows to the new mission as suggested by Father Camberos. But Father Vallejo, President of the eastern missions, was not at all pleased with quitting the mission at San Augustine. He admitted the truth that the Indians had not yet submitted to pueblo life, but in the thirty-six years of their work there the Fathers had baptized one hundred and fifty-eight—some in the hour of death. At short intervals the Indians had been induced to leave their habitats and to live about the mission, and hence, there was hope that with sufficient supplies the Indians could be returned from their rancherias. And, too, in case of French invasion, the establishment of San Augustine would be of strategic advantage to the Spaniards. Father Vallejo pleaded to the governor that Our Lady of Sorrows should be maintained even if with only one missionary. His point was carried. Our Lady of the Rosary Mission was authorized to remain as a separate foundation. Father Camberos had observed how impractical it was to congregate hostile tribes in the same mission. In language and in customs the Cujanes, Guapite, and the Karankawan differed from the Xaranames and Tamiques, who were living at Espíritu Santo, and they were not friendly. Since the Cujanes and their kindred had asked for a mission, and since it had already proved bad policy in other cases to transfer tribes to distant missions, Father Camberos thought that a separate mission was the only solution.

He went to Zacatecas, the headquarters of the Zacatecan missions, to make known his plan. In February, 1754, the guardian of the college appointed him to carry out his plan and sent him on to Mexico to seek authorization. He returned to Texas with authorization, but with no funds. In November he set to work to build a church. Private gifts to the college of Our Lady of Guadalupe of Zacatecas, and donations to the missionaries and of Captain Manuel Ramírez Piszina, commander of the presidio at Bahía, made the building possible. Bolton believes that "almost on the site" of modern Goliad Our Lady of the Rosary Mission was placed. Captain Piszina described the church as better than the presidio or the Mission of Espíritu Santo. It was placed in the midst of spacious plains and very fine meadows, and, in Piszina's estimation, its country was the best yet discovered in those parts, and had all the advantages neccessary for a large settlement. It had dwellings for the fathers and other offices. The church was a wooden structure finished within two months and made decent for divine worship. Some of the mission furniture was borrowed from Espíritu Santo. It was about four years before the government gave material aid to Rosary Mission.

Progress from the missionary point of view was slow. The Indians of this mission were very savage. They were intractable and on account of the shortage of supplies, it was sometimes advisable to let them roam. Father Camberos was conservative in administering baptism and in the first four years only twenty-one had been baptized and these were judged to be on the point of death, nine of whom were infants. In 1758 there was only one baptized Indian living at Rosario. In 1768 there was a total of two hundred baptisms. This, however, compares favorably with the records of the best missions in Texas.

In the diary of his tour of inspection in 1768, Father Gaspar José de Solís of Zacatecas makes the following observation of Mission Nuestra Señora del Rosário:

> The opinion I have formed of this mission of Nuestra Señora del Rosário is as follows: As to material wealth it is in good condition. It has two droves of burros, about forty gentle horses, thirty gentle mules, twelve of them with harness, five thousand cattle, two hundred milch cows, and seven hundred sheep and goats. The buildings and the dwelling, both for the ministers and for the soldiers and the Indians, are good and adequate. The stockade of thick and strong stakes which protects the missions from its enemies is very well made. The church is very decent. It is substantially built of wood, plastered inside with mud, and whitewashed with lime; and its roof of good beams and shingles (taxamanil) looks like a dome (parece arteson). Its decoration is very bright and clean. It has sacred vessels, a bench for ornaments and utensils, a pulpit with confessional, altars, and all the things pertaining to the divine cult. Everything is properly arranged and kept in its place. There is a baptismal font with a silver shell, and silver cruets for the holy oils. The mission has fields of crops, which depend upon the rainfall, for water cannot be got from the river, since it has very high and steep banks, nor from anywhere else, since there is no other place to get it from.
>
> This mission was founded in 1754. Its minister, who, as I have already said, is Fr. Joseph Escovar, labors hard for

The Zacatecan Missions (1716-1793)

its welfare, growth, and improvement. He treats the Indians with much love, charity, and gentleness, employing methods soft, bland, and alluring. He makes them work, teaches them to pray, tries to teach them the catechism and to instruct them in the rudiments of our Holy Faith and in good manners. He aids and succors them as best he may in all their needs, corporal and spiritual, giving them food to eat and clothing to wear. In the afternoon, before evening prayers, with a stroke of the bell he assembles them, big and little, in the cemetery, has them say the prayers and the Christian doctrine, explains and tries to teach them the mysteries of our Holy Faith, exhorting them to keep the commandments of God and of Our Holy Mother Church, and setting forth what is necessary for salvation. On Saturday he collects them and has them repeat the rosary with its mysteries, and the *alavada cantado*. On Sundays and holidays, before mass, he has them repeat the prayers and the doctrine and afterwards preaches to them, explaining the doctrine and whatever else they ought to understand. If he orders punishment given to those who need it, it is with due moderation, not exceeding the limits of charity and paternal correction; looking only to the punishment of wrong and excess, it does not lean toward cruelty or tyranny.

The Indians with which this mission was founded are the Coxanes, Guapites, Carancaguases, and Coopanes, but of this last nation there are at present only a few, for most of them are in the woods or on the banks of some of the many rivers in these parts; or with another nation, their friends and confederates, on the shore of the sea, which is thirteen or fourteen leagues distant to the east of the mission. They are all barbarous, idle, and lazy; and although they are so greedy and gluttonous that they eat meat almost raw, par-boiled, or half-roasted and dripping with blood, yet, rather than stay in the mission where the father provides them everything needed to eat and wear, they prefer to suffer hunger, nakedness, and other necessities, in order to be at liberty and idle in the woods or on the beach, giving themselves up to all kinds of vice, especially lust, theft and dancing.[6]

Such is the story of Rosary Mission up to 1768. In later years a stone mission was built and a pueblo was established near by. In 1793 the viceroy, Revilla Gigedo, included Rosary Mission in his letter to the Spanish Court. The site of its ruins is still pointed out to visitors of Goliad.

---

[6] Solís' *Diario* in the *Memorias of Nueva España* (xxvii, 256–259), cf. Dunn, "Founding of the Last Spanish Mission in Texas," in the *Southwestern Historical Quarterly* (xxv, 176).

6. Nuestra Señora de la Luz (1756).

In the summer of 1756, Jacinto de Barrios y Jáuregui, who was then Governor of Texas, began plans for a presidio and mission on the Trinity River as a barrier to further French encroachments. A site was selected at El Atascosito, above Orcoquisac near the north line of Chambers County, and a mission was established, dedicated to Our Lady of Light.

Little is known of the history of this mission. "Whatever chance for real prosperity it might have had," writes Bolton, "was destroyed by the continued uncertainty regarding a change of site and by the boisterous career of the nearby presidio. As was usually the case at new missions, at the outset the Indians were friendly, and they aided the Fathers in the construction of buildings and the planting of crops. Until 1758 the missionaries worked without the customary *ayuda de costa*, or initial subsidy, and had to depend for support on the governor. In June, 1757, Father Chavira died from the unhealthiness of the place, and his companion sought asylum at Los Adaes. In the following year two new missionaries were sent from the College, provided with the necessary outfit. By the time of Chavira's death the mission had completed a fairly substantial wooden church, plastered with clay and moss. Later this structure was replaced by a better one. The Indians were docile as a rule, but there is no evidence that they ever actually submitted to mission discipline of the kind enforced at San Antonio and on the Rio Grande."[7]

The two missions—Rosario and de la Luz—were not successful. In a report made in 1761 by Fray Simon Hierro, the guardian of the Zacatecan College of Guadalupe, we find the admission that practically all the Zacatecan missions had not prospered. Fray Hierro writes: "And, in truth, if we had not taken note of the fact that the Son of God in his gospel does not command us to convert, but only to preach, and that according to the Apostles the work of conversion is not that of the one who plants nor of the one who waters, but only of God, who gives the increase, it would have been an intolerable toil of forty years without that fruit that might have been reaped elsewhere . . . for, in all these years, if the time has not been altogether lost, it is because in

---

[7] Bolton, op. *cit.*, pp. 77–78.

The Zacatecan Missions (1716–1793)

the fulfillment of the divine decrees they have sent many infants to glory by means of holy baptism." Bolton continues: "The Indians had never consented to live in a mission pueblo, and there was not sufficient force to coerce them. Accordingly, there was no discipline in crafts or doctrine, and the only baptisms performed were administered *in articulo mortis*."[8]

So long as the Indians, by nature and instinct nomadic, could not be brought to live within the mission itself or on mission lands, there was little opportunity to teach them or to train them for permanent conversion to the Faith. The strongest evidence of the sad lot of the friars lies, as we have seen, in the fact that the only baptisms were those given *in articulo mortis*.

The first missionaries sent to la Luz Mission were Fathers Bruno Chavira and Marcos Satereyn. Father Chavira died within a short time and his place was filled by Fray Francisco Caro, formerly of the Los Dolores Mission among the Ais. From the Mexican documents in his possession, Bolton has drawn the following interesting facts of the story of the Mission la Luz: "The Indians of the place were not always docile, and there is no evidence that they actually entered the mission and submitted to its discipline. In 1759, during some trouble, the Attacapa joined the Orcoquiza in an outbreak, and in order to pacify them it was necessary to shoot a soldier. The trouble was evidently caused by one of the ever-recurring instances of misconduct on the part of the presidial soldiers. Slight as is our information before 1760, we are in possession of even less for the period between that date and the coming of Captain Pacheco, in 1764. But the occurrences at the time of his advent indicate that few Indians were living in the mission before that time, and that the mission building was in the state of decay when he arrived.

"This was, however, but a temporary wave of enthusiasm, lasting only a few months. The scandalous quarrel which ensued before the year was over between Pacheco and Governor Barrios, resulting in the flight of the former and his absence during the next five years, removed the best support of the missionaries, and there was a recurrence of former conditions at Nuestra Señora de la Luz, which the Marqués de Rubí, after a visit in 1767, referred to as 'an imaginary mission'."

---
[8] *Ibid.*, pp. 100–101.

Governor Barrios was not pleased with the choice the Zacatecan superiors had made. He found Father Chavira too old, and Father Satereyn too young. Father Vallejo, the president of the Zacatecan missions, listened to the governor's complaint and promised to remove the Fathers. But the unhealthful conditions of the lower Trinity country were too much for poor Father Chavira's feeble physique, and he died there on June 27, 1757. As for Father Satereyn, Governor Barrios changed his opinion of him and he was not moved, but later he took refuge from the malarial conditions to Los Adaes, Louisiana. Another Zacatecan friar came to fill the place made vacant by the death of Father Chavira. This was Father Francisco Caro, who had at one time been stationed at San Augustine at the Our Lady of Sorrows Mission. Father Caro was not impressed with the outlook at Our Lady of Light. In February, 1758, he wrote to Father Vallejo to complain of the unhealthful state of the place. Mosquitoes, bad water, excessive humidity and putrid lagoons made the site unfit for human habitation. His companion, Father Satereyn, and the soldiers were not well. He suggested moving the mission to El Atascosito, a point about forty odd miles up the Trinity. If this could not be done, Father Caro had one alternative. That was abandonment. Father Vallejo favored the transferring of the mission up the Trinity and in a letter to the governor he threatened to withdraw his priests if something were not done. What notion Governor Barrios may have gotten from Father Vallejo's threat is not clear, but he made a gesture of complying. He ordered crops planted at El Atascosito and told Del Rio, the lieutenant in charge, to make the transfer. Later he expressed himself as of the opinion that the new place was unfit for a colony. Father Joseph Abad de Jesús María came upon the scene in 1759 and took charge of the mission.

Unfortunate for the progress of Our Lady of Light Mission was the continuous uncertainty of the permanency of its site. From its foundation in 1756 to its abandonment in 1771 the question of transfer was unsettled. Father Abad seems to have had an attachment to the place. At any rate, he opposed the transfer and argued to the viceroy that it was laziness rather than unfitness of the site that retarded developments at the mission. It was in the mind of the Spanish authorities to establish a Span-

The Zacatecan Missions (1716-1793)

ish villa. The importance of the site took on a new significance. The new Governor, Don Angel Martos y Navarrete, was much concerned about a location. He made tours of inspection going as far west as Santa Rosa. Governor Barrios had surveys made of Santa Rosa in the Fall of 1756 and he had recommended the establishment of a villa and three missions around Santa Rosa.[9]

Governor Martos opposed Santa Rosa and likewise El Atascosito which Father Caro had suggested. He was favorably impressed with sites called Los Horconsitos and Los Pielagos which were seven to ten miles north of El Orcoquisac, the sight of our Lady of Light. Father Abad remained unchanged, though he had accompanied the Governor to El Atascosito. Father Vallejo had already expressed himself in favor of a transfer, but Governor Martos now inquires to find out whether the President of the mission still thinks a removal is imperative. Father Romero was consulted and was emphatic in his opinion for transfer. But the opinion of Father Vallejo and Father Romero does not change Father Abad's notion. In view of the uncertainty of what was best to do in face of these conflicting views, Governor Martos on request was relieved of the responsibility of locating a villa, at least, until a site could be determined. This indefinite action was taken by the viceroy in 1760. In 1762 a *junta de guerra* approved Los Horconsitos (Little Forks) and Martos was ordered to make the transfer. Between orders and their execution there oftentimes was great delay in early Texas. Nearly two years later Father Calahorra, a veteran missionary around Nacogdoches and now President of the Zacatecan missions in Texas, came in June, 1764, to aid in bringing about the transfer to the Little Forks. Del Rio, who had been branded as an incompetent commander by Father Abad some five years previously, had been replaced by Don Rafael Martínez Pacheco. This new commander of the presidio with Fathers Salvino and Aristorena had aroused a little interest on the part of the Indians in mission activity. Owing to the vacillating policy in regard to a transfer of site hardly anything of a missionary nature had been accomplished. Captain Pacheco found even the mission building in a state of decay. He assembled about one hundred and fifty Orcoquiza, passed the peace pipe among them,

---

[9] Bolton identifies Santa Rosa as the present town of Dustin or Houston (cf. *ibid.* p. 350).

addressed them in the presence of the Fathers, by an interpreter, Del Rio, informed them of the duties of neophytes, telling them that they must obey the king's officers and the missionaries, throw away their idols, attend prayers, work in the fields, live in the mission and defend it against attack. The Indians expressed their willingness to enter upon mission life and the next day they turned over to the Fathers their idols. Within three weeks Chief Canos and Chief Tomás came to obtain missions for their tribes. In face of this revival it is not surprising that Father Calahorra was unable to effect the transfer.

Captain Pacheco stood better with the Indians than he did with his soldiers. Father Calahorra checked a mutiny that was brewing on his arrival in June, 1764. But in October, trouble broke out and the torch was applied to some of the buildings in order to rout Pacheco. There is no evidence that the mission was threatened by the flames.

In September, 1766, a storm came in from the Gulf of Mexico and did some damage. After this it seems that the presidio was moved to higher ground close by. Our Lady of Light Mission was not changed. In 1767 the Marqués of Rubí found the mission still at El Orcoquiza. He recommended that the place be abandoned, and it is not likely that a transfer was ever made from that year until Father Ignacio María Laba and his companion retired after the presidio was deserted in 1771. The diligent search of Dr. Bolton found no evidence that the notion of Father Abad did not prevail. Our Lady of Light remained to the end on the hill where Father Abad said it stood in 1759, commanding "a view of the whole site of the presidio and of a circumference to the west and south where this River Trinity turns, as far as the eye can reach."

Storm, overflow, mutiny, and indecision were the great enemies of this enterprise. Captain Pacheco was forced to flee. The missionaries lost their best friend. Had Pacheco remained he would likely have brought the Indians to live on the reservation and the Zacatecans could have had more than "thirty perfect conversions" as a reward of their labors. The Zacatecan Friars, Romero, Chavira, Satereyn, Abad, Vallejo, Calahorra, Salvino, Aristorena, Silva, Marenti, Laba, Anselmo García, and Rosário Soto spent some time at Our Lady of Light Mission. Father Chavira died, and, was likely buried there. In the history of

The Zacatecan Missions (1716–1793)

Our Lady of Light come the names of such Indian chiefs as, Calzones Colorados, Boca Floja, Tamoges, El Gordo, Canos, Mateo, and Tomás of the Bidai tribe. Orcoquisac, Attacapa, Bidai, and Asinai Indians came in contact with the mission. These tribes occupied territory extending at least as far west as Spring Creek (Arroyo de Santa Rosa) and to the Neches River on the east, and from the coast on the south to the region around Nacogdoches on the north. Up to the present time the region in the valley of the lower Trinity has not made as much progress as has been made west of Nuestra Señora de Aranzazu, another name for the San Jacinto. There is a speculative interest in what might have happened in the vicinity of Houston if the plan for establishing a villa of Spaniards and of Tlascaltecan Indians had carried.

7. Nuestra Señora del Refugio (1793).

St. Francis of the Texans was the first of the missions to be established in the Querétarans' plan to Christianize the natives north of the Rio Grande. The last missionary foundation of the Franciscan Fathers in Texas was dedicated to Our Blessed Mother under the title of Our Lady of Refuge. This was a Zacatecan establishment. It was erected near the junction of the San Antonio and Guadalupe rivers (*a la parte del Oriente*). January 31, 1793, saw the beginning of this mission, though the viceroy had given his consent to the plan on December 31, 1791.

It is worthy of note that the spirit of Venerable Father Antonio Margil de Jesús lived on through this foundation. His name and his devotion to the conversion of the tribes dwelling north of the Rio Grande receive honorable mention in the letter addressed to the viceroy by Father Manuel de Silva begging the customary governmental support of the project. On August 11, 1790, Father Silva was elected Commissary and Prefect of the Zacatecan missions. Recalling the repeated charges of Father Margil to the sons of the Zacatecan College not to "yield to any difficulty" in the apostolic ministry in the "Provincia de los Texas," he resolved "as the first duty for fulfilling the obligation of my office, and to carry out so commendable charges which the Venerable Father Antonio Margil de Jesús left to our College, to enter personally in company with Father Lector Francisco Garsa [Garza] to see and to inspect that vast Province and to make an account of what would conduce to the advancement of its conquest, or of that which would retard or impede it . . . in order to attain the end so much desired, the conversion of those nations."[10]

Some three months after he was elected Commissary and Prefect of the missions, Father Silva set out for Texas in company with Father Garza. In January, 1791, they arrived in San Antonio. Father Silva felt the responsibility of his office and the urge of the saintly zeal of Father Margil, the first Zacatecan superior to establish missions in Texas. Since 1767 the harvest of souls in Texas was left exclusively to the Zacatecan friars. Father Silva found San Antonio relatively well organized. The missions of Rosário and Espíritu Santo caused him more concern. The barbarous condition of the unhappy Karankawas made special appeal to his zeal. He sent converted Indians from Rosário into the coastal prairies to inform these savages that his was a friendly purpose. Their welfare was Father Silva's motive. At length, in response to an invitation which the Karankawa delivered in person to Father Silva, he and Father Garza went to visit the Indians in their habitats. He was pleased with the opportunity to make a survey of the field which Father Margil had loved so well, but official duties left him little time. In the spring of 1791 he had to return to Mexico to preside at a chapter of his confrères.

Fortunately, he had a capable priest to leave in charge of the work initiated. Father Francisco Garza had spent some time in eastern Texas as chaplain of the Spanish settlement at the town of Nuestra Señora del Pilar de Bucareli. He had come to this town from San Antonio de Valero, probably in 1776; certainly, he was at the pueblo when disaster forced the settlers to take refuge to Nacogdoches in 1779. By correspondence and otherwise Father Garza had helped to lay the foundations of modern Nacogdoches. In 1783 he left Nacogdoches and became president of the Zacatecan missions in Texas. Other honors came to him among his fellows; he was made Lector in Sacred Theology and was a member of the Council of his college at Guadalupe, Mexico. But in the purpose of our story the greatest honor came to him in the spring of 1791.

---

[10] Father Silva to the viceroy in Audiencia de Guadalajara, 104–1–1.

The Zacatecan Missions (1716-1793)

It was he who selected the site and gave the title to Nuestra Señora del Refugio at the junction of the San Antonio and the Gaudalupe rivers. This was in the spring, probably in June, 1791. The following fall he went again to visit these Indians. He found the Indians' desire for a mission had increased. "If you build a mission at the mouth of the Guadalupe River, the whole coast is yours," one of the chiefs told him. It was more than two years later before he was able to begin the last of the missions. On January 31, 1793, he began the erection of Mission Our Lady of Refuge on the site selected and named by himself in the spring of 1791. He was assisted in the construction by Father Mariano Velasco. To this latter priest and not to Father Garza belongs the honor of being the first regular pastor.

Father Silva came to Texas in August, 1793, and found Father Velasco working faithfully at Our Lady of Refuge mission. Lowlands, mosquitoes, and discontented Indians made a removal of the mission advisable. The site chosen by Father Garza and approved by the soldiers and the Indians did not prove well adapted for the purpose of the Fathers. On January 10, 1795, they abandoned Father Garza's site and later transferred the mission some twenty-five or thirty miles south of the garrison of Espíritu Santo. This took them to a section known as Aranzazu or Santa Gertrudis. But the same title was given to the mission. Our Lady of Refuge still survives in the name of the modern town of Refugio. In the vicinity of this place was the last establishment of the missionary efforts of the Franciscans.[11]

The Zacatecan Fathers from the College of Our Lady of Guadalupe seem to have been partial to the Blessed Virgin in naming their missions. Our Lady of Guadalupe at Nacogdoches, Our Lady of Sorrows at San Augustine, Our Lady of the Rosary near Goliad, Our Lady of La Candelaria on the upper Nueces River, and Our Lady of Refuge in the vicinity of modern Refugio were Zacatecan establishments. Our Lady of Light was the invocation the Zacatecans selected for the mission on the lower Trinity.

---

[11] "Founding of the last Spanish Mission in Texas," in the *Southwestern Historical Quarterly*, xxv, pp. 174-184.

CHAPTER VI.

THE QUERÉTARAN—SAN FERNANDIAN MISSIONS *(1757-1769)*

The third apostolic college—College de San Fernando de Mexico—was founded in the capital city in 1734. It was from San Fernando that the Franciscans set out for Alta California, in 1768, under their celebrated President, Father Junípero Serra.[1] During the previous decade, the Fernandians had joined with the Querétarans in establishing three missions in Texas: Mission Santa Cruz de San Sabá, in 1757; Mission San Lorenzo, in 1762; and Mission Candelaria, in 1762. These three foundations were in the Apache country. The first foundation of San Sabá lasted but a year. San Lorenzo was given up 1769, and Candelaria in 1766.

"Whatever had been accomplished in the western district of Texas," says Bolton, "had been in the face of serious Indian depredations." In fact, side by side with the story of Franciscan progress in all those parts of Texas where they had founded missions, goes a chronicle of constant raids by savage Indian tribes, of martyrdoms both of Indian neophytes and of the friars, and of pillage. The principal tribe with which the Spaniards found themselves constantly at war was the Apaches. Wherever possible presidios were erected near the missions, and from these garrisons at times the soldiers were obliged to drive attacking parties of Indians, bent on outrage and murder.

About 1730 a change became apparent in the attitude of some of the Apache tribes, and the frequent forays into their country gave the Spanish officials and priests a better knowledge of how these savages might be approached. From reports printed in Bolton's *Texas in the Middle Eighteenth Century*, it is evident that the fierceness of the Apache attacks was due in large measure to the cruelty displayed by the Spanish soldiers upon their people.

According to a contract entered into between Don Pedro de

---

[1] Engelhardt, *Missions and Missionaries of California*, II, pp. 653-655.

The Querétaran—San Fernandian Missions (1757-1764)

Terreros and the Franciscans, it was agreed that the missions would be alternately erected by Querétaran and San Fernandian friars. Therefore the first San Sabá Mission (1757) was founded by the Querétaran Father Alonso Giraldo de Terreros, the cousin of Don Pedro, who brought to San Antonio in December, 1756, two priests from his own college in Querétaro and two from the College of San Fernando. These Querétaran priests, accompanying Father Terreros, were Fathers Joachín de Baños and Diego Ximénez, while the Fernandian Fathers were José Santiesteban and Juan Andrés.

Owing to the Comanche uprising, in which Father Terreros and Father Santiesteban were killed at San Sabá, the mission was abandoned about a year after its founding.

Among the tribes which seemed more friendly disposed were the Lipan Indians, who dwelt between the San Sabá and Rio Grande Rivers. Plans were often made by the Franciscans of San Antonio to erect a mission in the Lipan country, but it was only in 1757 that actual operations began. Captain Diego Ortiz Parrilla and Father Alonso Giraldo de Terreros were placed at the head of the San Sabá enterprise, and the mission was founded that year.

1. *Mission Santa Cruz de San Sabá (1757).*

This mission was established on the San Sabá River, near the present town of Menardville, Texas. It was intended to serve the Apache Indians. Almost from the very beginning of the settlement at San Antonio in 1718, this fierce tribe of Indians had made themselves known to the Spaniards. In spite of their treacherous nature or rather, likely, because of it, the Apache became objects of the special zeal of the Franciscans, who accompanied military campaigns against the Apache and tried to induce these savages to adopt Christian ways and civilized life. On one of these campaigns a lay-brother, Fray Pita, was murdered somewhere between the Brazos and the San Gabriel River about the year 1722. Soon after the transfer of the Querétaran missions from East Texas to San Antonio a pitched battle was fought with the Apaches a short distance from San Antonio, in the year 1731. The following year Governor Bustillo y Zevallos journeyed to the northwest as far as a river which Dr. Bolton is inclined to think, was the San Sabá. He had for his campaign a body of Christian Indians, whose presence was doubtless due to the zealous notion of the Franciscans that the Apache might be drawn to Christianity by the example of Christian Indians. At any rate it was the custom of the Fathers to make use of their converts in trying to persuade others to Christian living. Certainly they were never satisfied with the efforts of the soldiers. In 1740 Father Santa Ana, President of the San Antonio missions, expressed in no uncertain terms his dissatisfaction. "If," he said, "the campaigns were conducted with more discipline and with a better and more disinterested purpose, it would not be difficult to secure peace with them (the Apache) in their own country. . . . Of what took place in the present campaign Rev. Father Fray Felipe will give a good account. I can only say that it is very important that others like it should not be made, for neither God nor the King gains anything, while the hatred of the Indian is increased, the peace of the Province in this way becoming more disturbed. On account of the unseasonable time when the campaign was made, and the disorders which the soldiers were allowed to commit, many were left so heavily in debt that for a long time to come they will have nothing to eat or to use; the expedition was profitable only for those who had horses and other goods they sold at excessively high prices; and it is ridiculous that these same persons should claim certificates as servants of the King our Lord, when they were interested in what I have stated, and had greater hopes for considerable prizes of horses, hides, and Indian men and Indian women to serve them. These are the purposes of the campaigns and the ones entertained by most of the citizens who join the soldiers in such operation; and since the purpose is so vile, so is the outcome."[2]

Five years after writing this opinion, Father Santa Ana went with Captain Toribio Urrutia into the Apache country beyond the Colorado. Some of the Indians were taken captive. It was the policy of the Franciscans to use kindness with these captives who were held as hostages. The kindly spirit of this Franciscan policy bore some fruit even in the hearts of these savages. The captives themselves became more tractable under the treatment of the Fathers and in some cases their tribesmen were touched

---

[2] Cited by Bolton, *op. cit.*, p. 271.

The Querétaran—San Fernandian Missions (1757-1764) 67

with appreciation. The Lipans, a branch of the Apaches, had even asked for a mission. Missionaries were not wanting in their willingness to go. Some years previously, Father Francisco Hidalgo, famous for his persisting love for these unhappy natives of Texas, asked to go alone, except for the company of a laybrother, to labor for the conversion of the Apaches.

By reason of the happy relations existing with the soldiery during the captaincy of Toribio Urrutia, the Fathers were not so retarded in their influence for good among the Apaches. The horrors of war against these Indians were tempered with more mercy. In 1749 Father Mariano de los Dolores y Viana accompanied Urrutia on an expedition of retaliation against the Apache. Though there was considerable provocation Father Mariano succeeded in persuading the Spaniards not to kill even one Apache. Father Mariano knew that this was appreciated by the savages. Later he sent an embassy of peace to the Indians in the person of an Apache woman who had lived as a hostage around the San Antonio missions. She had come to know the benign influence of the Franciscans and she succeeded in winning over her people to sue for peace. They were warmly welcomed by the Spaniards. A peace banquet was prepared for them; beef, corn, squashes and fruits were the menu. Preceding the discussion of peace, the Franciscans saw to it that the Holy Sacrifice of the Mass was offered. The following day, at the instance of Father Santa Ana, all prisoners of war were set free. The next day, August 19, 1749, the City of San Antonio witnessed a great disarmament ceremony. In the center of the plaza a hole was dug and the implements of Apache warfare were interred therein. It is needless to say that the war-weary Franciscans were pleased with this peace demonstration of the Lipans. For thirty years, in journeys, labors, prayers, and by diplomacy, they had striven earnestly to sow the seed of the Gospel in the region of the Apaches. This sincerity gave the Fathers hope that the seed was about to take root in the hearts of the Lipans. A short time previously Father Francisco Xavier Silva died at the hands of the Natages, another branch of the Apache Indians. But the death of this zealous Zacatecan, as well as that of his eight soldier-companies, did not shatter the hopes that the Fathers had in the Lipans. Father Mariano de los Dolores urged an establishment for them on the banks of the Guadalupe; Father

Santa Ana thought it would be better to place the mission on the Pedernales River, nearer Apachería.

The Fathers agreed in their desire; they did not agree in the best means of realizing that desire. Further investigation was deemed necessary; delay ensued. In 1753 Father Aranda was sent with Lieutenant Galván on exporation. The former reported on his return that he had gone as far as the San Sabá, had found good land, stone, and wood; he was received with affection by the Indians, and saw them venerate a cross which he bore in procession, praising God and His Most Pure Mother. Father Aranda and Lieutenant Galván selected a site and made their recommendations for a mission. Father Mariano had been instructing and even baptizing Lipans earnestly pleading for the sacraments at San Antonio. He had no doubt of their sincerity, and emphasized this fact in a letter to the viceroy strongly confirming the report of Father Aranda. But further exploration was ordered. In December, 1754, Father Juan López under the protection of Captain Rábago was sent to the San Sabá. These two returned approving Paso de la Cruz, the site of Father Aranda and Lieutenant Galván. But delay was still the policy of the vice-regal authorities. Rumors of rich mineral deposits in the district of Apachería had been reaching the ears of the government officials. Another investigation was conducted under the direction of Bernardo de Miranda in 1756 by order of Governor Barrios. Some of the reputed silver ore came to the hands of Don Pedro Terreros. He was a citizen of Mexico, a man of means, a trusted friend of the Querétaran Fathers, their *sindico* at the college in Querétaro. Distinguished amongst the Franciscans was his cousin, Father Alonso Giraldo de Terreros. Don Pedro came forth with a scheme that was to establish the Franciscans amongst the Apache, at least, an opportunity was to be given them to try out their desires and hopes in behalf of these Indians.

Don Pedro submitted a plan to the Fathers of the College of Holy Cross, at Querétaro. He offered the munificent sum of $150,000 to be used in establishing and maintaining missions to the number of twenty for a period of three years among the Apache. The Queréterans felt that they had not sufficient men for so great a number of missions. They suggested that every second mission established be entrusted to the care of the Fathers of the College of San Fernando of Mexico City. This was satisfactory to Don Pedro, and for the first time this college comes into the story of the Church's history in Texas. Hitherto the College of Holy Cross, at Querétaro, and that of Our Lady of Guadalupe, at Zacatecas, had been supplying the laborers for this section of the Lord's vineyard. Magnificent as was this offer, four months of deliberation were required before its final acceptance. The enterprise was put under the direction of Father Alonso Giraldo de Terreros. Santa Cruz College appointed Fathers Joachín de Baños and Diego Ximénez, and San Fernando College entrusted its share in the work to Fathers José Santiesteban and Juan Andrés. In company with nine families of Tlascaltecan Indians from Saltillo, the missionary band arrived at San Antonio in December, 1756.[3]

Omens were not propitious at San Antonio. Delay on the part of Colonel Diego Ortiz Parilla in military command of the project, and disappointment on the part of Father Mariano de los Dolores y Viana of the sad San Xavier project, must have tried the patience of Father Terreros. Wisdom, prudence, and executive ability had characterized his administration at San Juan Bautista on the south bank of the Rio Grande and had led his superiors to place him in charge of the Querétaran responsibilities in Texas.

Undaunted by opposition he persisted in his firm resolve to persevere. The winter was spent at San Antonio in securing stock and supplies for the mission. In the spring messengers were sent to the Apaches in the vicinity of San Antonio to invite the Indians to come to meet the missionaries. Father Terreros was joined by Father Mariano in distributing gifts to those who answered the invitation. The Indians were happy with the outlook and promised fidelity. In April, 1757, the departure for San Sabá was made.

On the south bank of the San Sabá River near the present town of Menardville, Menard County, Texas, the Mission of Holy Cross was erected soon after their arrival in the latter part of April, 1757. Three or four hundred persons were in the presidial settlement. But sorrowful for the missionaries no Indians were to be seen. They sent out embassies and in June about three thousand Lipans put in their appearance. Danger from

---

[3] Arricivita, *op. cit.*, p. 366–368; Bolton, *op. cit.*, p. 85.

the Comanches was impending and the Lipans could not be induced to stay. Other bands came and went. A cloud of discouragement began to settle down over Holy Cross Mission. Little opportunity was afforded the Fathers for spiritual administrations. Three of them departed. Father Terreros, and Father Santiesteban were the only two of the original remaining in March, 1758. They had been joined in the preceding January by Father Miguel Molina of the San Fernando college. He stayed until the bitter end came, on the Feast of Our Lady of Sorrows, March 16, 1758.

Father Terreros said Mass at daybreak on March 16. After finishing Mass, he was distracted by the wild cry of Indians and the discharge of firearms. It is not hard to imagine his sentiments on beholding his mission church surrounded by some two thousand Comanches, mounted on horses and armed with French guns. One of the Spanish guards recognizing a Texas Indian, thought that the visit was a friendly one. On the force of his assurance Father Terreros went out to meet the band. The Indians feigned friendship and pretended to desire an alliance with the Spaniards. The missionaries began to distribute gifts of tobacco and other things to the Indians. But the Fathers had their misgivings, for as soon as the Indians gained entrance into the stockade they began to plunder whatever struck their fancy. The Fathers realized their helplessness. Their only hope was conciliation. The Chief asked Father Terreros to accompany him to the presidio which was about three miles up the river on the other side. Father Terreros consented after a Texas chief pretended that he had been unsuccessful in his effort to approach the presidio. Father Terreros, who had labored so well and so long among the Indians, realized that he was in danger. In spite of the danger he mounted a horse and proceeded to direct the Texas chief to the garrison. As he was leaving the enclosure about the mission a gun-shot rang out and Father Terreros fell to the ground, mortally wounded. His pitiful condition made no appeal to the barbarous Comanches. They rushed upon him viciously, put him to death, and tore his holy habit from his body. A general assault was under way. They rushed into the buildings and came upon Father Santiesteban. Mad in their fury they quickly dispatched this good friar who had come from San Fernando College to spend his life for the good of the Indian. Father Molina was in another room and in the company of a brave soldier, accurate in his aim. The Indians were unable to make immediate approach to Father Molina who escaped to tell the tale later to Father Francisco Palóu who has recorded the story of Father Molina in his biography of Father Junípera Serra. Father Palóu describes the scene as follows:

> The Indians also discharged their weapons and a bullet penetrated the arm of the Father (Molina) and he lived carrying it there for many years. The valiant soldier was badly wounded in the legs from the bullets, but even wounded as he was he killed many and defended the Father until night, when the pagans retired. Seeing that he was so seriously wounded and no longer with strength either to defend the Father or to attempt to run away, and understanding that he had but a short time to live, he insisted on the Father's leaving him and trying his fortune in getting away in order to carry the word to the garrison. . . .
> The Father was afraid to go out when he saw that the Indians had built fires about in order to easily discern what they were doing, and although he thought they would kill him as soon as they saw him, he none the less decided to go, and trusting in God and in the Most Holy Mary (whose Sorrows Holy Church is wont to celebrate on that day) he crawled out through a window and was enabled to pass between two of the bonfires without being seen. He threw himself in the river and floated down stream and then made his way, not by the trail lest he should be found, but through the woods to the garrison where he arrived three days later, bleeding and fainting for the lack of food, as he had nothing to eat but the raw herbs of the field and had dared to travel only by night. He recuperated in the garrison and the captain immediately sent troops, but when they arrived at the place the Indians had already gone away, after having burned up everything including the body of the dead soldier, who, as Father Molina himself afterwards said (and it was he who told me the whole story), had wounded and killed no less than forty of the pagans.[4]

The Comanches remained at the scene of their slaughter three days, withdrawing on August 20, 1758. Father Terreros and Father Santiesteban were buried side by side near the site

---
[4] Palóu, *Life of Serra*, p. 40; cf. Arricivita, *op. cit.*, pp. 386–389. (For the deaths, p. 377.)

of the burned remains of Mission Santa Cruz, probably in a section that was reserved for a cemetery. Two soldiers were buried with them and six other soldiers were buried where they had fallen.

Father Terreros had planned his work with customary Franciscan enthusiasm. Long experienced in missionary activities, he laid out the Holy Cross mission in the form of a square, had erected a spacious building of poles and thatch for a temporary church, placed similar buildings as a residence for the Fathers, barracks for the soldiers, and store houses for supplies, and, as a reminder of his earnest hopes, crops were growing on plots of ground near the mission. Holy Cross Church had a short existence. But it was a noble effort of a noble soul.[5]

2. *Mission San Lorenzo (1762)*.

Following upon the deaths of the Querétaran Father Terreros and the Fernandian Father Santiesteban at the San Sabá mission, much confusion and conflict of ideas prevailed among the Spanish authorities. Parrilla, the officer in charge of the San Sabá project, proposed a complete abandonment of the work among the Lipans. The Franciscans were opposed to this in spite of the great loss they had suffered. It was after a long period of endeavor that they had entered upon the conversion of the Apache, for even death in the service of the missions lost much of its horror for a Franciscan. The death of Father José Santiesteban, the first of the sons of the College of San Fernando to offer his life in Texas, served but to increase the determination of the Fernandians. Immediately on hearing of the catastrophe, the superior of the missionaries of this college appointed no less a person than the great Father Junípero Serra to take up the work where his confreres had fallen. But owing to delay and confusion on the part of the government, this able priest was diverted to other work, eventually becoming in California one of the outstanding missionaries of all time. Texas lost the imprint of his character which is ineffaceably written and revered in California's glorious missionary history. Father Serra's companion in Texas was to have been Father Francisco Palóu. In 1750 Father Serra was made superior of a mission at Santiago, where

---
[5] Arricivita, *op. cit.*, pp. 375–378.

he remained for nine years with Father Palóu as companion, and Father Serra's great work in California is better known by reason of the faithful chronicles of his companion and biographer, Fray Francisco Palóu. Holy Cross College of Querétaro then appointed Fathers Francisco Aparicio and Pedro Parras for the San Sabá field. Don Pedro de Terreros continued his generous support of the missionaries despite the futility of his first venture, which resulted in the death of his cousin, Father Terreros.

Following the destruction of the Santa Cruz Mission in March, 1758, several military campaigns were ordered and executed by the government officers. These resulted chiefly in failure and eventually in supplanting the commander of the presidio on the San Sabá, Colonel Diego Ortiz Parrilla, with Captain Felipe Rábago in October, 1760. Rábago's name was in bad repute with the Querétarans around San Antonio for some of them, as we have seen, held him in complicity with the murder of Father Jose Ganzábal at Mission Candelaria on the San Gabriel River in 1752.[6]

Finding Lipans around Fort San Luis de Las Amarillas who were willing to enter into mission life, Rábago appealed not to San Antonio but to Father Diego Ximénez, president of the Rio Grande missions. Father Ximénez visited the San Sabá district, made extensive investigations, selected suitable sites, returned to the Rio Grande, and in the fall of 1761 made known his plans to his superiors. This investigation and report of Father Ximénez led to the establishment of the Mission San Lorenzo.

In its origin San Lorenzo was another Querétaran establishment. Father Ximénez and Father Joachín de Baños were the representatives of the college of Querétaro. They were the original appointees to accompany Father Alonso Giraldo de Terreros to his ill-fated charge at Mission Holy Cross. Fortunately they were absent when the Comanche raid came, March 16, 1758. January 23, 1762 found them back among the Lipan-Apaches at a place called El Cañon. Dr. Bolton locates this site about seventy miles to the southeast of Father Terreros' mission of the San Sabá district. It was on the east side of the Rio de las Nueces, according to an observation in the diary of Nicholas La Flora, an engineer on Marqués de Rubí's tour of

---

[6] Cf. Bolton, op. cit., p. 54.

inspection of the year 1767. Apparently it was either on the eastern border of Edward's County or the western border of Real County.

Poles and brushwood were gathered around El Cañon and by January 23, 1763, a temporary church was in order. Standing in the door of the structure, Father Ximénez and Father Baños sounded a bell and some three hundred Indians came. Vested in alb and stole Father Ximénez blessed the place and a cross which had been erected. In his bare feet he went with great solemnity to venerate the cross before the eyes of the curious on-lookers. Captain Rábago was present and to him was given the honor of carrying the cross to the Altar in the church. Holy Mass was celebrated and the *Alabado*[7] was sung. The Church of San Lorenzo had an almost fruitless existence. It was founded at El Cañon at the request of the Lipans then fearful of the Comanches. This unsettled state of mind continued and little good was done by the missionaries towards Christianizing and civilizing their charges. The Spanish soldiers had all they could do to contend with the Commanches and other wild tribes. The presidio was maintained at San Luis Amarillas until Rábago thought it wise to retreat to El Cañon in 1668. In the meantime the small number of soldiers in garrison at San Lorenzo were of inconsiderable aid to the Fathers. They could not keep the Lipans on the reservation. Hence the Fathers' influence on the savages was of little consequence. Their services were judged "unprofitable" by Nicholás La Flora on his trip through El Cañon, in 1767. He found Father Rivera and another Father Santiesteban at the Church of St. Lawrence. The inference is that Fathers Ximénez and Baños had been replaced. In 1769 the presidio was withdrawn still further to the southwest, this time going to San Fernando de Austria below the Rio Grande. This brought an end to the Church of St. Lawrence of the Holy Cross. The sands of Apachería were shaken from the sandals of the Franciscans. Arricivita sums up their story thus: "All the fruit of the eight years of toil and sufferings, consisted of eighty baptisms administered to the Indians at the point of death, and of the few children offered by their parents for Baptism at the beginning of the missions. Nevertheless, the Fathers departed with the lamp of Faith burning brightly in their hands,

---
[7] See pp. 85–86.

charity still alive in their hearts, compassion in their souls, zeal in their labors, meekness in their countenances, poverty in their garb, quite resigned to the cruel adversities that they had borne so long among such ungrateful, decitful, greedy, vagabond barbarians, whom they could in no manner convert nor even raise to the grade of catechumens."[8]

3. *Nuestra Señora de la Candelaria (1762).*

The third of the Apache group of missions was established by the Fernandians a short time after the founding of San Lorenzo de Santa Cruz and was placed eight or ten miles farther down the Nueces River to the South of El Cañon, on the opposite side of the stream. Captain Rábago intended this mission to serve the Apaches who were then under the leadership of Chief Turnio. The title of this last foundation among the Apaches leads us to surmise that it was founded around the feast of Candlemas, February 2, 1762. As we have seen, by the terms of the gift of Don Pedro Terreros the Fathers of the college of San Fernando in Mexico City were to take a share in the work of christianizing the Apaches. According to Nicholás La Flora, La Candelaria consisted of a house "with a little chapel, and in front of it a large thatched house which the Lipanese built, flattering the Fernandian missionaries that they would submit to live in a settlement, but they never did so, and only mocked their zeal and credulity."[9]

It is not at all doubtful that the Fernandian Fathers were able to read Indian character at least equally as well as La Flora, and perhaps the disappointment of having to leave La Candelaria in about four years' time after its foundation was not a surprise to the zeal of the Franciscan missionaries. The true cause of the outcome of the mission was due to the wild nature of the Apache who could not be tamed in face of persistent war with his enemies, the Comanches and other savage tribes.

The work of San Lorenzo and Candelaria Missions did not continue long. Bolton says that San Lorenzo lasted almost seven years (1762-1769) and that Candelaria was abandoned in

---
[8] *Op. cit.*, p. 389 translated by Engelhardt in *Missionary Labors etc.*, July, 1917, p. 263.
[9] Cited by Bolton, *op. cit.*, p. 95.

1766. "Their existence was precarious and their results extremely meager. The Indians were fickle, deserted at will, and returned mainly if at all to get food and presents. For this they could hardly be blamed, for they were soon pursued to their haunts by northern tribes, and suffered frequent massacres in the very neighborhood of the missions."[10]

The end of the missions in eastern and western Texas was not far off, and before the process of secularization had begun in 1793, naught apparently was left except the missions in and around San Antonio. These, too, were to be taken from the control of the friars within the next two decades. But to offset the decline in Texas there is the outstanding successe of the San Fernando friars in California after 1768 under Serra and his successors.

In the *Four Decades of Catholicism in Texas,* we read that "the missionary period of Texas history was fraught with earnest efforts, noble deeds, and heroic sacrifices. It rose, flourished and declined a century previous to the establishment of the Catholic hierarchy in the United States. At its decline there was ushered in a new era, more political and economic than religious, whose importance threatened to overshadow and even blot out the vestiges of a hundred years of trial and endeavor. The ruthless hand of time, the ravages of war, and the corrosive forces of nature shared in consigning the missions to oblivion."[11]

The action of the government in suppressing the missions began on January 2, 1793, when a decree was issued for the secularization of San Antonio de Valero. Secular priests were assigned to take the places of the Franciscans. The following year (April 10, 1794) all mission centers in northern and eastern Texas were secularized. In 1813, the Spanish Cortes passed a general law to the effect that all the mission lands should be abandoned to the civil authorities. The revolution in Mexico which had already broken out when this order was issued lasted till 1821, and by that date all the remaining missions, with the exception of Refugio were suppressed. This was followed by the action of the Mexican government (September 5, 1823), which brought the history of Franciscan effort in Texas to a final close.

---

[10] *Ibid.,* p. 94
[11] *Op. cit.,* p. 1.

CHAPTER VII.

THE ADMINISTRATION OF THE MISSIONS

There was nothing which set apart as distinctive the missionary methods of the Franciscans who came to Texas from the three Apostolic Colleges of Querétaro, Zacatecas, and San Fernando. In fact in many cases, there was mutual coöperation and only on rare occasions do we find anything but friendly rivalry between the presidents of the three groups of friars. The method of founding a mission, the style of buildings erected, the system of catechetics employed, the crafts and trades taught the Indians, and the regulations followed in the admission of the Indians to Baptism, were practically all alike in the twenty odd Texas mission centers. The same abuse of power on the part of the civil authorities and the same moral and religious problems created by the type of Spanish soldiery in the presidios are in evidence in all the mission history. The friars of all three colleges had the same type of enemies. The same difficulties that hindered and thwarted the success of the missionaries can be traced everywhere.

There were, naturally, owing to individual tastes and tendencies, certain divergencies which set off Zacatecan from Querétaran, and Querétaran from Fernandian methods. But in general the history of the administration of any one mission is the history of all. One difference, however, should be noted: the architecture of the missions displays various stages of progress toward the harmonious design visible in the California missions or in those which are still standing in and around San Antonio.

The founding and administration of the missions forms a part of the general narrative of Spanish conquest of the lands north of the Rio Grande. Each mission was more than a religious center for the conversion of the natives. It was part of the general penetration of civil administration into the province. Politically, Texas was a buffer state between New Spain and the French colonial empire which had been erected on both sides of the Mississippi and from the unknown regions of Canada and the Gulf of Mexico.

"As an administrative unit," writes Bolton, "Texas was a part of the Kingdom of New Spain. In civil and military affairs the province was subject directly to the viceroy and to the Audiencia of Mexico, and in ecclesiastical matters to the archbishop of Guadalajara. The government of Texas, apart from the mission, was almost wholly military. The villa of San Fernándo de Béxar, the only civil community in the province, had its own cabildo and a modicum of self-government. The official head of the province was the governor. He held his office by royal appointment; *ad interim governors* might be appointed by the viceroy. The governor was *gobernador* and *captain general* of his province and captain of the presidio of Los Adaes, the capital. All important matters of administration, such as the founding of new missions, new presidios, and new colonies, or the making of military campaigns, were referred directly to the viceroy. He in turn customarily sought the advice of the fiscal of the Royal Audiencia and the *auditor de guerra*. In case these two functionaries disagreed, or in matters of unusual moment, a *junta de guerra y hacienda*, composed of leading officials of the the different branches of the administration was called. In all matters of importance the decisions of the viceroy were made subject to royal approval, but it frequently happened that the act for which approval was asked had already been performed. In ordinary affairs of provincial adminstration the fiscal and the *auditor de guerra* really controlled the government. Checks upon the governors were provided through *Visitas*, or inspections, and through the *residencia*, or investigation, at the end of the governor's term. As a rule the *residencia* was formal, but sometimes, as in the cases of Sandoval and Barrios, investigations were serious matters.

"In the half-century between 1731 and 1780 Texas had thirteen governors and governors *ad interim*. The average term of office was about four years, but it varied from a few months in the case of Boneo y Morales to about eight years in the cases of Barrios y Jáuregui, Martos y Navarrete, and Ripperdá. As a rule the governors were professional soldiers. Orobio Bazeterra had been a merchant at Saltillo; Winthuisen and García Larios seem also to have been civilians. Martos y Navarrete had been a naval officer with the rank of *teniente de navío*. The rest were soldiers. Two of them, Bustillo and Sandoval, came to Texas with the rank of captain. Of the others, two were lieutenant-colonels, four were colonels, and one a general. Some of the men were of high social rank. Boneo y Morales was a Knight of the Order of Santiago. Barrio was *alcalde provincial* of the Santa Hermandad of all New Spain, and Ripperda was a baron. On the whole, judging by its occupants, the office of governor increased in importance, and its military character was emphasized as time went on.

"Not only were the men professional soldiers, but they belonged also to what might be termed a class of professional office-holders. In several cases they came from governorships and were sent to others after serving in Texas. Bustillo was promoted to the office from the captaincy of the presidio of La Bahía. Sandoval and Martos had been governors of Coahuila, and Barrios of Nuevo León; Franquis held the office while waiting for the governorship of Tlascala. After leaving Texas, Barrio returned to the governorship of Nuevo León; Barrios went to that of Coahuila, and Ripperdá became governor of Comayagua in Central America. Oconor became *comandante inspector* of the interior provinces. Probably none of the governors were great men, but, being placed on a military frontier with slender forces, they had little opportunity to distinguish themselves in the only field where distinction was possible. Their contemporary renown depended much upon the views of partisan writers.

"The administration of Texas, as of the other provinces, was corrupt with 'graft.' The positions of governor and presidial commander were made attractive largely by the opportunity which they afforded for making money in addition to the fixed salaries. The pay of soldiers was made chiefly in food, clothing, and equipment, purchased by the governor and commanders, and charged to the presidial soldiers at enormous profits. Thus the post of governor or captain was scarcely less that of a merchant than soldier. To give a single example, it was charged that in the eight years of his incumbency Governor Martos y Navarrete made over $80,000 in profits on the goods which he sold his company at Los Adaes, not to mention his gains from trade with Indians, missions, and French neighbors and from his private stock ranch, all conducted, without private expense, through the labor of his soldiers.

"The government of New Spain was highly centralized in

theory, but the effects of the centralization were greatly lessened by the fact of distance. Through the right of petition, which was freely exercised, the local leaders in the frontier province of Texas often exerted a high degree of initiative in government, and, on the other hand, through protest and delay they could and frequently did defeat mandates of the higher authorities."[1]

Owing to the close and intimate connection between Church and State in Spanish lands at that epoch, the success of the missions depended almost entirely upon the harmony of the relations between viceroys, governors, and captains on the one hand, and the Franciscan presidents and friars on the other.

"Considering the importance of the church," writes Smith in his *The Viceroy of New Spain*, "it is not a little surprising that there was so little conflict between it and the state, but whatever the reason for this may have been, there can be no question that the relations of the State and Church in Spanish America were free from serious conflicts, even if these relations were not always exactly harmonious."[2]

The actual administration of the missions, however, was entirely in the hands of the friars and their ecclesiastical superiors. Relation with State officials were on the whole peaceful until the end of the Spanish regime; but there were a number of outstanding minor points of friction, which were seldom settled and these had a share in the lack of triumph in the Texas missions. As Smith has pointed out, "the almost perfect harmony between the clergy and the civil government during the last days of Spanish rule will help to explain the extreme loyalty of the Church to the Spanish government, when the war of independence broke out."[3] We have an instance of this in the attitude of the friars of the California missions during the rebellion raised by the ex-priests Hidalgo and Morales in 1811-1815.[4]

---

[1] Bolton, *Texas in the Middle Eighteenth Century*, pp. 6–7. Cf. Austin, Mattie Alice, "The Municipal Government of San Fernándo de Béxar, 1730–1800," in Texas State Historical Association *Quarterly* (VIII, 277–352); Jones, Garfield, "Local Government in the Spanish Colonies as Provided by the *Recopilación de leyes de las Indias*," in *Southwestern Historical Quarterly* (XIX, 65–90); Blackmar, F. W., *Spanish Institutions in the Southwest*, Chapter VIII.

[2] P. 229.

[3] *Ibid*.

[4] Engelhardt, *Missions and Missionaries etc.*, II, 650–651.

Engelhardt lays down the general principle for an appreciation of the mission system and the administration of the religious center of the Franciscans, when he asks the reader to bear in mind the object which they wished to accomplish. "The method," he writes, "naturally resulted from the purpose in view, and this was none other than the conversion of the savages to Christianity. The friars came as messengers of Christ. Their message was the Gospel as preached by Christ and His Apostles. Like the Apostles they had severed every tie that interfered with the delivery of this message. They had given up relatives, friends, property, prospects, and mother-country for the sake of attracting souls to Christ. They paid little or no attention to questions of things that could not aid them materially in gaining the good will of the people whose salvation they had at heart. Like the Apostles, the Franciscans came not as scientists, geographers, ethnographers, or school-masters, nor as philanthropists eager to uplift the people in a worldy sense to the exclusion or neglect of the religious duties pointed out by Christ. Superficial writers and shallow pedagogues have found fault with the early missionaries for not emphasizing what they are pleased to call 'education'; but, inasmuch as the friars came in the spirit of the Saviour and of the Apostles, they saw no need of laying stress upon such knowledge save in so far as it helped them to gain their end. In this they but followed the example of the Divine Master. Christ surely could have given the most lucid and effective instructions on worldly education and all other subjects that agitate the learned and unlearned of every period. Nevertheless He urged but the one thing necessary. He sent out His disciples merely to preach what He had told them."[5] Indeed the administration of the missions must remain a closed book to those who refuse to understand that the principal object of the friars was to impart the truths of the Catholic Faith.

This aim did not exclude the work of education of the Indians, nor did it close the eyes of the friars to the fact that the missions represented Spain and Spanish conquest as well. Bolton writes:

> The missions, like the presidios, were characteristically and designedly frontier institutions. From the standpoint

[5] *Ibid.*, II, pp. 242–243.

of the Church the principal work of the missionaries was to
spread the Faith, first, last, and always. But the missions
were agencies of the State as well as of the Church, and
were supported by the government to serve the State's purposes.
As viewed by the government, the work of the missionaries
was to assist in extending, holding, Christianizing, and
civilizing the frontiers. By going among the outlying tribes
they were often most useful explorers and diplomatic agents.
By gaining an influence over their neophytes, they counter-
acted foreign influence among them, deterred them from in-
vading the interior settlements, and secured their aid in
holding back more distant tribes. But the Spanish policy
looked to the civilizing of the Indian as well as to the holding of the frontier, and it saw in the mission the best possible
agency for bringing this about. Since Christianity was the
basic element of European civilization, and since it was the
acknowledged duty of the State to extend the Faith, the first
task of the missionary was to convert the heathen. But
neither the State nor the Church in Spanish dominions considered the work of the missionary ending here. If the
Indian were to become either a worthy Christian or a desir-
able subject he must be disciplined in the rudiments of civilized life. Hence the missions were designed not only as
Christian seminaries, but also as so many industrial and
agricultural schools.

The central feature of every successful Spanish mission
was the Indian pueblo, or village. If he were to be disciplined, the Indian must be kept in a definite spot where
discipline could be imposed upon him. The settled Indians,
such as the Pueblo Indians of New Mexico, could be instructed in their native towns, but the wandering or scattered tribes must be assembled and established in pueblos,
and kept there by force if necessary. To make the Indians
self-supporting as soon as possible, and to afford them the
means of discipline, the missions were provided with com-
munal lands, for gardens, farms, and ranches, and with workshops in which to practice the crafts. Religious instruction
and industrial training were imparted by a definite routine
of tasks, prescribed by the superior and authorities but administered with much practical sense and regard for local
circumstances.

Designed as frontier institutions, the missions were intended to be temporary. As soon as his work was done on
one frontier, the missionary was expected to pass to another.
In the theory of the law, within ten years each mission was
to be turned over to the secular clergy and the common
lands distributed among the Indinas. But this law was
based upon experience with the civilized natives of central

Mexico and of Peru; on the northern frontier, among the barbarian tribes, a longer period of tutelage was always found necessary.

As a rule the annual stipend (Sinodos) of the missionaries, $450 each, was paid by the royal government, which bore also the initial expense of founding a mission (*ayuda de costa*). A marked exception to this rule was the munificent gift of Pedro de Terreros in 1757 for the support of missions among the Apache. The stipends were spent by the *sindicos* of the respective colleges for annual mission supplies (*avios*), which were sent to the frontier by mule trains in charge of lay brothers, acting in the capacity of conductors of supplies.[6]

The procedure of founding a mission was simple enough. Usually, a spot was selected near a river, high enough to be protected from floods and sufficiently guarded against high winds. A cross was placed at the site chosen for the church. Rude huts for the missionaries, the soldiers, and their attendants were built. Later structures were raised on the patio system. When sufficient supplies and money reached the friars the work of building the church and of the other structures was begun.

"Besides the church," Bolton says, "each mission had its *convento*, or monastery, including cells for the friars, porter's lodge, refectory, kitchen, offices, workshops, and granary, usually all under common roof and ranged around a patio. At San Antonio de Valero the *convento* was a two-story structure fifty varas square with two patios and with arched cloisters above and below. That at San Francisco de la Espada had seven cells, four above and three below; at San Juan there were five cells.

"An important part of their training was the workshop, for here the neophytes not only helped to supply their economic needs but got an important part of their training for civilized life. At each of these four missions the Indians manufactured *mantas, terlingas, sayales, rebosos, fresadas,* and other common fabrics of wool and cotton. At Mission San Antonio the workshop contained four looms and two store rooms with cotton, wool, cards, spindles, etc. At Concepción and San Francisco there were three looms each; at San Juan the number is not stated.

---

[6] *Op. cit.*, p. 10.

"The neophytes of each mission lived in an Indian village, or pueblo, closely connected with the church and monastery. Of the four Queréteran missions we have the fullest description of San Antonio de Valero. It consisted of seven rows of houses built of stone, with arched porticoes and windows. There was a plaza through which ran a water-ditch grown with willows and fruit trees. Within the plaza was a curbed well to supply water in case of a siege by the enemy. The pueblo was surrounded by a wall, and over the gate was a tower, with embrasures, and equipped with three cannon, firearms, and munitions. The houses were furnished with high beds, chests, metates, pots, kettles, and other domestic utensils. The pueblo of San Antonio was typical of all. At Concepción there were two rows of houses, partly of stone, partly of thatched straw, surrounded by a wall. At San Juan the houses were of thatch, but preparations were being made to replace them with stone structures. For defence the mission had two swivel guns, twenty muskets, and, presumably, a wall. At San Francisco the pueblo consisted of three rows of houses.

"Agricultural and stockraising activities had increased since 1745. At the four Querétaran missions there were now grazing 4,897 head of cattle, 12,000 sheep and goats, and about 1,600 horses, and each mission had from thirty-seven to fifty yoke of oxen. Of the four missions San Francisco raised the most stock, having 2,262 head of cattle and 4,000 sheep and goats. San Juan came next, and Valero next. At each establishment maize, chile, beans, and cotton were raised in abundance, besides a large variety of garden truck. At the time when the report was made (March 6) each of the missions had in its granary from 1,600 to 2,000 bushels of maize, and a corresponding stock of beans. Each mission had well tilled fields, fenced in, and watered by good irrigating ditches with stone dams. Each had its ranch, some distance away, where the stock was kept, with one or more stone houses, occupied by the families of the overseers, the necessary corrals, farming implements, carts, and tools for carpentry, masonry, and blacksmithing."[7]

When all was ready for occupancy, a solemn religious service was held and the friars began in a systematic way to attract

[7] *Ibid.*, pp. 97–99.

The Administration of the Missions

the Indians to the mission. Curiosity brought the earliest comers, and gifts of food, clothing, and trinkets induced others to approach the mission. Above all, the real attraction was the gentle manner of the missionaries, their anxiety to be of assistance in the smallest detail to the savages, and their methods of rewarding those who showed a reciprocal feeling. Obviously the first requisite to reach the Indian mind was to know his language. To some extent classes in some of the Indian dialects were given at the colleges of Querétaro and Zacatecas, and the friars did not come totally unable to make themselves understood. But a grave difficulty faced the priests at the outset of each mission and that was the multiplicity of the dialects spoken in any given locality. "It was impossible," writes Engelhardt, "for the missionary to learn all the languages of his mission. Apart from the royal mandate which required that the Spanish language should be taught and spoken among the neophytes, it was therefore necessary to introduce a medium of communication in order that the Indians coming from different bands might be able to converse with one another. Thus it was that the Castillian became the universal tongue of the California Indians. This made it possible to instruct all the catechumens of a mission at the same time. Meanwhile the Fathers made use of interpreters who rendered instructions into Indian, or frequently taught the converts themselves. Several of the friars learned the dialect spoken by a majority of a mission, and then taught the neophytes in their own native idiom. However, interpreters continued a standing necessity, because new candidates for Baptism applied for admission who knew nothing but their own jargon. Changes also took place among the missionaries through death, or illness, or at the expiration of the statutory term of years in the service. Interpreters were therefore indispensable."[8]

The daily exercises were similar in all the missions, with certain minor changes necessary on account of the climate or the character of the Indians themselves. The whole mission was awakened by the bells which rang out at sunrise, and all the natives except the children under nine years, came to Mass, during which one of the friars recited morning prayers. At the end of Mass the invocation (*Alabado*): *Praised be the Most*

[8] *Op. cit.*, II, 252.

Holy Sacrament of the Altar, and the Immaculate Conception of the Blessed Virgin Mary, was sung by the all the friars and Indians. An instruction in Christian doctrine followed, and then came breakfast. Engelhardt, whom we are following here, gives a description of the rest of the day: "After breakfast, which lasted about three-quarters of an hour, the men and the larger boys went to the work assigned to the field, among the live-stock, or in the shops. The girls and single women found occupation under the care of the matron. At noon the Angelus bell announced the time for dinner. This was served in the same manner as the breakfast, but consisted of pozole, a gruel, to which meat, beans, peas, lentils, or garbanzos were added according to the seasons and means of the mission. Two hours were allowed for the meal and for rest. At two o'clock work was resumed, one of the missionaries encouraging the neophytes by his words and example. At about five o'clock work ceased, and the whole population went to church for the recitation of the "Doctrina" and religious devotions. On these occasions the Father would add an instruction in Spanish or Indian as appeared expedient for his polyglot audience. As usual the *Alabado* concluded the exercises. At six o'clock supper was served in the shape of atole. The remainder of the evening was passed in various amusements. In this matter the Indians enjoyed much latitude. They were permitted to indulge in the pastimes of their savage state as long as decency and Christian modesty were not offended."[9]

Sundays and holy days of obligation were times of repose. High Mass was sung and instrumental music by the Indians was the accompaniment to the plain chant. In the afternoon, the Rosary, Litany of the Blessed Virgin, and other prayers in Spanish were recited. There were suitable devotions for the various parts of the ecclesiastical year, such as the Way of the Cross in Lent. The civil officials were always anxious to have the Indians learn Spanish, knowing that the language would be a sure means of pacifying these lonely outposts of the colonial empire, but the friars realized that the surest means of teaching Christian virtue was in the respective dialects of the Indians, with whom they had to deal. Many of the friars learned these dialects, but for the most part interpreters were used.

[9] *Ibid.,* p. 254.

The Administration of the Missions

The "Doctrina Christiana" which was used for the instruction of the savages was recited in common by the neophytes. It contained the Way of the Cross, the Lord's Prayer, the Hail Mary, the Apostles' Creed, the Confiteor, the Precepts of the Church, the Seven Sacraments, the necessary points of Faith, and the Four Last Things. Engelhardt relates that as late as 1888 he heard the Sanel Indians near Hopland, California, recite the "Doctrina" in Spanish by heart.[10]

The principal occupation of the Indians in the missions was agriculture. After the land was cleared for a good distance on all sides of the mission, grain was sown and when necessary an irrigation system was installed. That at the missions of San Antonio is still a surprise to modern visitors. All the implements were of the crudest sort. In one of Engelhardt's descriptions of the farming system of the California missions, we have what may be accepted as a summary of the Franciscan administrative methods.

> The plough, which is still used in many districts of Mexico, was composed of two pieces of timber. One of these was formed of a crooked branch of such a shape that it constituted the sole and the handle or stilt. A sharp piece of iron was fitted to the point of the sole. The other piece was a beam of undressed timber long enough to reach the yoke which was fastened with thongs of rawhide to the horns of two oxen that drew the plough. This beam was inserted into the upper part of the main piece of wood on which it would slide, and which was fixed by two wedges. By withdrawing these wedges the beam was elevated or lowered, and by this means the plough was regulated as to the depth of the furrow. The plowman went on one side holding the handle or stilt with his right hand and managing the goad with the left. Only a rut could be made and the soil could not be turned over deep; this necessitated crossing and recrossing the field many times. A harrow was unknown. Where the wheat and barley were sown, a bushy branch was used to cover the seed. In places a log of wood for the axle was drawn over the field. Corn was planted by hand in the rut made by the plough, and the seed was covered with soil by means of the foot.
> Harvesting was similarly primitive and laborious; but as there was no need of haste it made no difference to the Indians, and the missionaries were satisfied to see their wards

---

[10] *Op. cit.*, Vol. I, p. 99.

acquiring habits of industry and shunning idleness. The grain was thrashed after a method which explains the command in the Old Testament, Thou shalt not muzzle the ox that treadeth out the corn on the floor. The cut grain was spread on a level spot of hard soil. Around this poles were driven into the ground so as to form a circle from about fifteen to twenty feet in diameter. Into this enclosure an Indian led a number of cattle, or preferably horses and mules. He would keep them moving about in the ring, and thus from the stamping the wheat was thrashed out. The chaff was thrown away, and the wheat was brought to the granaries in ox-carts or by mules. This simple method is still in use among the Pueblos of New Mexico.

The form of the carts was as rude as that of the plough. It was composed of a bottom frame of a most clumsy construction on which poles were stuck upright and connected at the top with slight bars. The wheels of the ox-cart were also of a most singular construction. They had no spokes, but were composed of three pieces of timber. The middle piece was hewn out of a tree of sufficient size to form the nave and the middle of the wheel all in one. This middle piece was made of a length equal to the diameter of the wheel, and rounded at the two ends to arcs of the circumference. The other pieces were made of timber naturally bent and joined to the sides of the middle piece by keys or oblong pieces of wood, grooved into the ends of the pieces which formed the wheel. The whole was then made circular, and resembled the wheels of barrows. Sometimes the wheels, two or three feet in diameter, were made of one block of wood. Into the construction of this cart no particle of iron, not even a nail entered, for the axle was entirely of wood, and the linch-pin of the same material, as well as the pins that fixed the cart to the axle. The pole was of large dimensions, and long enough to be fastened to the yoke in the same manner as the beam of the plough.

Wheat and corn were ground to flour by the Indian women after their own primitive way by crushing with the pestle in a mortar or in baskets. Later on water mills were introduced. They, too, were of the most primitive construction, Forbes informed us; but none better were found in other parts of Spanish America, not even in Chile where wheat abounded. These mills consisted of an upright axle, to the lower end of which was fixed a horizontal water-wheel placed under the building, and to the upper end of the mill-stone. As there was no intermediate machinery to increase the velocity, the mill-stone could make only the same number of revolutions as the water-wheel. This necessitated a wheel of small diameter, otherwise no power of water thrown

The Administration of the Missions

upon it could make it go at sufficient rate to give the millstone the requisite velocity. The wheel was constructed in the following manner: A set of so-called spoons were stuck into the periphery of the wheel which served in the place of float boards. They were made of pieces of timber in something of the shape of spoons; the handles were inserted into the mortises on the edge of the wheel; and the bowls of the spoons received the water which spouted on them and forced round the small wheel with nearly the velocity which impinged upon it.[11]

Besides agriculture, the Indians were taught various practical trades by the friars. Pottery, carpentry, and masonry, the making of shoes, hats, clothes, soap and candles, hide-tanning, spinning, and blacksmithing, are some of the handicrafts mentioned in the reports of the missionaries.

While it would not be historically accurate to state that the administration of the Texas missions can be completely learned from the description we possess of the Franciscan missions in California, nevertheless it must be remembered that the daily routine and other regulations observed in California were compiled by Father Pedro Pérez Mezquía, who till 1744, had labored in the missions of Texas, and afterwards in those of Sierra Gorda, Mexico, whence Father Junípero Serra introduced them to his beloved converts in the missions on the coast.[12]

This glorious picture is not without its shadows. The truth is that, unless the Indians were under contract by piece-work, he, or she, never worked unless a friar was present to direct the labor. All the year's toil on the part of the missionaries failed to eradicate the deepest of all the vices the Indian possessed— laziness—and the friars are not loath in their frank reports to the guardians of Zacatecas and Querétaro to admit that with many, if not with all, of their neophytes, the chief attraction was free food. "Nothing seemed to give them greater pleasure than to lie stretched out for hours upon the ground with their faces down, doing absolutely nothing and indifferent to everything."[13] Yet in spite of this general laziness, the friars did not neglect to provide amusements for the Indians. In fact, amusements of legitimate character had to be supplied in order to sup-

[11] *Ibid.*, II, p. 257–261.
[12] *Missionary Labors*, in the *Franciscan Herald*, June, 1916, p. 232.
[13] Bancroft, *Native Races*, I, pp. 393–394.

plant the Indian's passionate love for gambling of any sort. Many of these amusements were a kind of biblical representation or tableau or akin to the mystery plays of earlier ages.

The whole object of the missionaries in systematizing the daily life of the Indians was to make the mission so attractive that the neophytes would remain long enough to be instructed in Christian doctrine and so prepared for Baptism. As we have seen in describing the Texas missions, the friars were very careful never to baptize an Indian unless he gave promise of Christian stability. The fact that not so many were baptized when they were at the point of death reveals the almost insurmountable difficulty which met the missionaries at the very gate way of the sacramental life of the Church. From Espinosa's rare work, the *Chrónica Seráfica,* we learn that, "almost from the beginning the Fathers began to maintain themselves by the bread of tears and affliction. The first trouble occurred when seven of the twenty-five soldiers, who had been sent to guard the missions, deserted and abandoned us, at the same time taking along some of the animals destined for the use of the friars. After selecting the site of each mission, the missionaries assigned to them had to construct their little thatched dwellings unaided; and as no provisions were forwarded, abstinence commenced on the first day. Although it was not the season of Lent, the meals consisted of nothing more than a little purslane seasoned with salt and pepper. Once in a while the Indians would give us a little corn, a kind of bean, and some wild fruits, which served to divert rather than appease our hunger. Rarely was a mouthful of meat obtained. Once it happened that a goat fell sick from a sore leg. The animal was slaughtered, the leg cut off, and the remainder sustained us for more than a week. Chocolate, which usually went with the meals, was scarce; for we had received but fifty pounds which had to be divided amongst us five religious from Santa Cruz College. Fortunately, though all the Fathers had their troubles and suffered various hardships, they were able to celebrate Holy Mass every day, during which we supplicated the Lord most earnestly for the conversion of the Indian tribes.

"In proceeding to render an account of our apostolic labors, I must remark that the Indians lived very far apart. Our main efforts, therefore, were aimed at persuading them to unite and settle down in permanent villages. Although they gave us hopes of complying with our desires, when they gathered their crops, the various difficulties that arose were so great that during twenty years not one of the missionaries enjoyed the consolation of having all the Indians of his charge gathered at his mission. The few that did settle down were, therefore, removed to the more populous districts in order to induce the other Indians to congregate in large numbers; but generally not enough fertile land could be discovered for the maintenance of a thousand people attached to each mission. So the plan failed. The Fathers had to content themselves with visits from the natives. On such occasions the missionaries, who had already acquired a sufficient knowledge of the language, would endeavor to eradicate the erroneous notions of their visitors about religion, and would demonstrate the vital necessity of receiving the Sacrament of Baptism, after they had learnt and professed the truth of One God and Three Divine Persons. The poor natives, however, would appear unmoved or indifferent; for they were so attached to what they had inherited from their forefathers, that only with the divine assistance could the absurd superstitions, which grew up with them from their childhood, be rooted out of their hearts. This great obstacle was, indeed, learnt from one of their chief medicine men. At length, one of the Fathers succeeded in convincing him of the truth of the Catholic Faith to such an extent, at least, that the wily Indian could find no more arguments with which to oppose him. Thus cornered, he frankly admitted that the religious notions of the Indians had been merely inherited from their ancestors, and that this fact alone accounted for the tenacity with which the Texans clung to them.

"The women exhibit far greater willingness than the men to accept the truths of salvation. The happy consequence of this was that many of them had the good fortune of receiving holy Baptism on their death bed, when the priest would be called to administer the sacrament, which had always been postponed for want of security that the person while enjoying good health would comply with obligations the Christian Faith imposes.

"Among the little ones the desired fruit was gathered in abundance; for all those who died in their infancy only a few escaped the zealous vigilance of the missionaries, and so died without Baptism. In order that none of the chldren should miss the supreme happiness of dying in sanctifying grace, the Fathers made out a list of the huts and rancherias with the number of adults and children in each. Whenever an Indian came to visit the missionaries they would closely question him in regard to the health of his whole family. When they ascertained that any one was ill, they would express lively sympathy, and then immediately go to visit the sick person, in order to give the requisite instruction to the adult or to baptise the child discovered at the portals of death. This occasioned much hardship for the Fathers and they also met with great opposition at times on the part of the parents, who declared that the baptismal water deprived their children of life. The zealous missionaries generally disillusioned the poor people of these silly notions with the happy result that, moved by the grace of God, even many adults willingly received Baptism during their last illness.

"At times sickness became general among the natives. The malady most common among the Texans and which carried off most of them was dysentery. During the severe winters they were accustomed to throw heaps of live coals under the elevated bunks to moderate the great rigor of the cold. The consequence was that most of the Indians suffered from this disease. And had they not frequently bathed throughout the year, even when the ground was covered with snow, there would have been far more victims of over-heated blood. Whenever such an epidemic raged, the watchful missionaries did not wait to be called. As soon as they had celebrated Holy Mass, they would mount their horses and visit all the rancherias or villages and hamlets, and they would not return until they had baptized all those they supposed to be dying. If they met with resistance, they would repeat the visit on the next day, meanwhile entreating the Lord to open the spiritual eyes of the deluded Indian; and the good Lord, moved by his own benignity, since those poor creatures were bought by the price of His Blood, would facilitate the administration of Baptism.

"The hardship endured by the missionariess in their great zeal will be better understood, if the reader bears in mind that the ranchos of the Indians lay far apart; that some of them were situated six and even seven leagues distant in every direction. Hence, it was not an easy matter, even if the missionary galloped his horse, to visit the greater number of ranches in one day, especially when it became necessary to remain a long time instructing the dying, or persuading those in health not to prevent the eternal salvation of the sick."[14]

The value of this description is heightened by the fact that Espinosa, as President of the Querétaran missions, had a long active experience in the Texas missions.

Judged by modern standards of efficiency, the Texas missions were unhappy in their outcome. Probably the only exceptions were the San Antonio Missions which had lasted long enough to enable the friars to test their methods in various ways and to reach a surer means of holding the Indians to mission life. But outside these missions, the others in central and eastern Texas were too short-lived to prosper in spite of the heroic efforts of their founders. Changed as these missions were so often owing to the fear of French invasion and to invasions made by savage tribes, very little that was permanent could be begun. Certainly no success equal to the California missions can be predicated of the eastern and central Texan groups. And this fact is proved by the undoubted success of the Zacatecans and San Fernandians in the California groups.

In these missions, however, lies the beginning of Texas history. The ruins of the churches and the conventos, many now completely obliterated, are among the oldest monuments to the progress of the white man in the United States.

[14] *Chrónica Seráfica*, p. 439 (Engelhardt's translation).

CHAPTER VIII.

SOURCES FOR EARLY TEXAS CATHOLIC HISTORY (1690-1820).

When John Gilmary Shea, at the earnest suggestion of Jared Sparks, undertook to write a general history of the missionary efforts of the Catholic Church among the American Indians, very little had been published in English in that extensive and comparatively unknown field. This was in 1854. It is true that the work of Bancroft, Sparks, O'Callaghan, Kip, and others, had by that year revealed to some extent the heroic labors of our early missionaries. Many volumes had seen the light in Mexico, Spain, France, and elsewhere, dealing with American missionary history; and it was known that the civil and ecclesiastical archives of Mexico and Spain contained an almost inexhaustible number of documents for the colonial period of that part of New Spain which eventually formed the southwestern part of the United States.

Shea's *History of the Catholic Missions Among the Indian Tribes of the United tates (1529-1854)* was a revelation to American historians. The English and French missions were known, owing to the works of O'Callaghan, Sparks, and others; but in his chapters on the Spanish missions of New Mexico, Florida, and Texas and California, Shea brought to light hitherto untouched sources which had a profound influence upon the generally accepted theory of cruelty and tyranny in the conquest of New Spain. "Cruelties, indeed, were practiced," Shea writes, "but they did not form the general rule. The part taken by the missionaries, ever the steadfast friends of the Indians, has been singularly misinterpreted, and they seldom figure in English accounts unless as persecutors. Yet never did men more nobly deserve a niche in the temple of benevolence than the early and later Spanish missionaries." Shea's narrative is based upon all the available historical material of his day: Torquemada's *Monarquía Indiana*; Barcia's *Ensayo Chronológico*; Henrion's *Histoire générale des Missions*; Benavides' *Memorial*; Palóu's *Sérra*, and other general works. Evidently, Shea had not then (1854) seen the *Crónica Seráfica* of Espinosa and Arricivita, but he makes use of both these volumes in his *Catholic Church in Colonial Days (1521-1763)*, which was published in 1886. In fact, Shea's chapter on the Church in Texas (1690-1763) in this volume is built upon Arricivita, Morfi's (Manuscript) *Memorias para la Historia de la Provincia de Texas, los Documentos para la Historia Eclesiastica y Civil de la Provincia de Tejas*, Villaplana's and Guzmán's lives of Margil, the current histories of Texas, and various unpublished documents which he found in the Library of Congress.

From the date of the first volume of Shea's *History of the Catholic Church in the United States* (1886), very few works have been published in which further facts of Texas Catholic history were revealed. The volume of the *Catholic Encyclopedia* which contains the article on Texas was issued in 1912. This was from the pen of John F. O'Shea. Naturally in so short a space he was unable to add much to the colonial history of the Church in Texas, but his article contains a succinct account of the Franciscan missions within that State.

To one historian more than to any others, even including John Gilmary Shea, the Catholic Church owes an ever-increasing debt of gratitude for works of the highest scientific value in this field. To Dr. Herbert Eugene Bolton, of the University of California, countless historical students are indebted for a series of articles in the *Quarterly* of the Texas State Historical Association, the *American Historical Review*, the *Southwestern Historical Quarterly*, and in other reviews which have revealed the attraction that lies within the story of these Texas Franciscan Missions. In his *Guide to the Materials for the History of the United States in the Principal Archives of Mexico*, (Washington, D. C., 1913), Dr. Bolton has given to the historians of the southwestern section of the United States, a catalogue of all the principal documents dealing with Catholic activity in the hispanic territory which is now a part of our country. Here we find for the first time a list of manuscripts which contain the history of the three apostolic colleges of Querétaro, Zacatecas, and San Fernando, from which, as we have seen, the Franciscans from 1690 to 1793 came into the Texas missionary field. Supplementary to this splendid guide is the *Spanish Exploration in the Southwest (1542-1706)*, which Dr. Bolton contributed in 1916 to the

Original Narratives of Early American History. The third part of his *Spanish Exploration* contains: the original documents for the Bosque Expedition into Texas in 1675, in which Father Larios took part; those for the Mendoza Expedition of 1683-84 among the Jumano of Texas, in which Father Nicolás López figured; and those of the more important De León Expedition of 1689-1690, which brought to Texas the Franciscan to whom the title Founder of the Texas Missions has been given: Father Damian Massanet. All these documents, in particular the Letter of Father Massanet describing the founding of the Province of Texas, which was first published in 1899 in the Texas State Historical Association *Quarterly* (II, 253-312), and which is one of the most important sources of Texas history, have been used in this essay on the Franciscan Missions.

But beyond these works, Dr. Bolton has given us another volume, without which much of our knowledge of Franciscan activity in Texas would not be known—*Texas in the Middle Eighteenth Century,* which was published in 1915. For the period of Texas history beginning with 1731 down to the end of the eighteenth century, little that was accurate had been ascertained before Dr. Bolton began his study. The work itself is not a history in the strict sense of the term, but rather a collection of special studies with copious use of documentary material from the archives of Mexico, Spain, and Texas. For the most part, these documents are used by Bolton for the first time, and this fact will explain why we have cited the work so often. "The assembling of these materials," Dr. Bolton writes in his Preface, "during a period of thirteen years, has been the greater part of my task. My quest has been as romantic as the search for the Golden Fleece. I have burrowed in the dust of the archives of Church and State in Mexico City, in a dozen Mexican state capitals, in Natchitoches, Louisiana, and in numerous places in Texas. The distance travelled in my pursuit of documents would carry me around the globe. I have lived with the *padres* in ruinous old monasteries in out of the way villages in the mountains of Mexico. I count among the treasures of my personal archive the letters of introduction from ambassadors, secretaries of state, and governors; cardinals, archbishops, bishops, friars, and parish priests, who have smoothed my way.

Sources for Early Texas Catholic History (1698-1820)

"My researches have taken me not only into foreign archives in quest of records, but also over hundreds of miles of old trails in Texas, Louisiana, and other parts of the Southwest, in search of topographical and archæological data, for light on the historical tale. I have ridden by team long distances over the old San Antonio Road, where no railroads run, and on horseback in mud fetlock deep, over the historical trail from Natchitoches, the old French outpost of Louisiana, to Los Adaes, (now Robedine), the Spanish outpost of Texas. In a successful search for the lost San Sabá mine, I have ridden and tramped in the hills of Llano and the Colorado. To examine the ruins and map out the sites of the forgotten missions near Rockdale, I have several times driven and tramped back and forth, up and down the valley of the San Gabriel. But in the discovery of lost sites, I count as my cardinal joy the identification of the location of La Salle's fort, on the Garcitas River, near the shores of Lavaca Bay."

Two collateral works were found of special importance in our study of the missions. The first of these is by Anne E. Hughes, the *Beginnings of Spanish Settlement in the El Paso District*, which was written under Dr. Bolton's direction, and published in vol. I of the *Studies in American History* (1914). Basing her researches upon the documents discovered and made available by Dr. Bolton, Miss Hughes tells for the first time the authentic history of the Spanish settlements in the El Paso District. The second work which has guided us is William Edward Dunn's *Spanish and French Rivalry in the Gulf Region of the United States* (1678-1702).

To Dr. Dunn we owe several special studies which throw considerable light on the difficulties the friars met in Texas: *Apache Relations in Texas, (1717-1750), Missionary Activities among the Eastern Apaches Previous to the Founding of the San Sabá Missions,* and *The Apache Mission on the San Sabá River, Its Founding and its Failure*. The first two articles appeared in Texas State Historical Association *Quarterly,* (XIV, 198-274; XV, 186-200), and the third in the *Southwestern Historical Quarterly,* (XVI, 379-414).

To Father Zephyrin Engelhardt's four massive volumes—*Missions and Missionaries of California* (San Francisco, 1908-1915), all students of Catholic Church history in the old southwest and in California must turn for an accurate and detailed description of the aims and methods, the administrative regulations, and the actual working of the missions. But to Engelhardt in a particular manner is the historian of the Franciscan Missions indebted, since the venerable historian contributed some years ago (October, 1914—November, 1917) a series of articles in the *Franciscan Herald*, entitled *Missionary Labors of the Franciscans Among the Indians of the Early Days (Texas)*. These articles are based upon Bolton's *Texas in the Middle Eighteenth Century*, and upon the *Crónica Seráfica* of Espinosa and Arricivita.

While not within the years included in this essay, the *Four Decades of Catholicism in Texas, 1820–1860*, published by Sister Mary Angela Fitzmorris, Ph.D., (Washington, D. C., 1926) is helpful for the much confused period of the secularization of the Missions (1793-1820). Sister Angela's work is based mainly upon the San Antonio Archives, now housed in the County Court House of San Antonio, upon the Lamar, Nacogdoches, Bexar, and other unpublished papers in the Texas State Library and the Library of the University of Texas.

Kirwin's *History of the Diocese of Galveston* (Galveston, 1922), contains a good description of the missions of Texas, as well as an unpublished paper by the late Monsignor W. W. Hume on the Venerable Margil de Jesús.

For the earlier period of Franciscan missionary history the recent (1916) publication by William Edward Ayer of the *Memorial of Fray Alonso de Benavides (1630)* is especially valuable since it contains (pp. 187-285) a series of excellent notes by two prominent scholars in the field of Spanish-American History—Frederick Webb Hodge and Charles Fletcher Lummis.

The basic works for any study of the Texas Missions are the two rare volumes: Espinosa's *Chrónica Apostólica y Seráfica de Todos los Colegios de Propaganda de Fide de Esta Nueva España*, printed in Mexico, 1746; and the *Crónica Seráfica y Apostólica del Colegio de Propaganda Fide de la Santa Cruz de Querétaro en la Nueva Epaña, Dedicada al Santisimo Patriaraca el Señor San Joseph*, Segunde Parte, by Father Juan Domingo Arricivita, which forms the continuation of Espinosa's works, and which was printed in Mexico in 1792. Fortunately, these volumes have been available in the Library of Congress.

Sources for Early Texas Catholic History (1698-1820) 99

Bancroft's *History of the North Mexican States and Texas* (2 vols., San Francisco, 1883-1889), were found to be of little value for this essay. In fact, Bancroft practically ignores the work of the missionaries.

Of the larger histories of Texas, those which gave direction to our researches were: George P. Garrison, *Texas, a Contest of Civilizations*, (Boston, 1903), and Dudley Wooten, *A Comprehensive History of Texas, 1685-1897*, (2 vols., Dallas, 1898).

Added to these is the incomplete but valuable *Catalogue of Franciscan Missionaries in Texas (1528-1859)*, published by Rev. Edmund J. P. Schmitt, at Austin, 1901.

Bibliographical lists on Texas will be found in Fitzmorris *Four Decades of Catholicism in Texas, 1820-1860*, (pp. 101-104), in Bolton *Texas in the Middle Eighteenth Century*, pp. 449-453), and in Dunn, *Spanish and French Rivalry in the Gulf Region of the United States, 1678-1702, Austin, 1917*. Raines has compiled a catalogue of works in his *Bibliography of Texas*, (Austin, 1896).

The following list of books and or articles in current historical and literary Reviews will give an indication of activity shown by students in the colonial history of Texas. Many of them were found to be of minor help for our subject, but all contain valuable data:

Austin, Mattie Alice. *The Municipal Government of San Fernando de Bexar, 1730-1800*, Texas State Historical Association *Quarterly*, VIII, 153-170.
Baskett, James Newton. *A Study of the Route of Cabeza de Vaca*, in Texas State Historical Association *Quarterly*, X, 246-280.
Binkley, William Campbell. *New Mexico and the Texas-Santa Fe Expedition* in Southwestern Historical *Quarterly*, XXVIII, 85-108.
Bolton, Herbert Eugene. *Athanase de Mézières and the Louisiana-Texas Frontier, 1768-1780*, 2 vols. Cleveland, 1914.
  Location of La Salle's Colony on the Gulf, in Southwestern Historical *Quarterly* XVII, 171-190.
  Native Tribes About the East Texas Missions in Texas State Historical Association *Quarterly*, X, 246-280.
  Some Materials for Southwestern History in the Archivo General de Mexico in Texas State Historical Association *Quarterly*, VI, 103-113.
  Spanish Mission Records at San Antonio, in Texas State Historical Association *Quarterly*, X, 297-308.
  The Jumano Indians in Texas, 1650-1771 in Texas State Historical Association *Quarterly*, XV, 66-85.
  The Spanish Abandonment and Reoccupation of East Texas in Texas State Historical Association *Quarterly*, IX.
  The Founding of Mission Rosário—A Chapter in the History of the Gulf Coast, in Texas Historical Association *Quarterly*, X, 113-140.

The Spanish Occupation of Texas 1519–1690 in *Southwestern Historical Quarterly*, July, 1912 (Reprint).

Tienda de Cuervo's Yinspeccion of Laredo, 1757, in *Texas State Historical Association Quarterly*, VI, 187–204.

Buckley, Eleanor Claire. *The Aguayo Expedition into Texas and Louisiana, 1719–1722*, in *Texas State Historical Association Quarterly*, XV, 1–65.

Casis, Lilia M. *Descumbrimiento de la Bahía Del Espíritu Santo*—Damian Manzanet. Translation, in *Texas State Historical Association Quarterly*, II, 252–281.

Clark, Robert Carlton. *Louis Juchereau de Saint-Denis and the Re-Establishment of the Tejas Missions*, in *Texas State Historical Association Quarterly*, VI, 1–74.

The Beginnings of Texas, Austin, 1907.

Cox, Isaac Joslin. *Educational Efforts in San Fernándo de Béxar*, in *Texas State Historical Association Quarterly*, VI, 27–64.

Father Edmond John Peter Schmitt, in *Texas State Historical Association Quarterly*, V, 206–212.

The Louisiana-Texas Frontier, in *Texas State Historical Association Quarterly*, X, 1–76.

The Early Settlers of San Fernándo, in *Texas State Historical Association Quarterly*, V, 142–161.

Dunn, William Edward. *Apache Relations in Texas, 1717–1750*, in *Texas State Historical Association Quarterly*, XIV, 198–274.

Missionary Activities Among the Eastern Apaches Previous to the Founding of the San Sabá Missions, in *Texas State Historical Association Quarterly*, XV, 186–201.

Spanish and French Rivalry in the Gulf Region of the United States, 1672–1702. Austin, 1917.

The Apache Mission on the San Sabá River, Its Founding and Its Failure, in *Southwestern Historical Quarterly*, XVI, 379–414.

García, Fr. Bartholome, O.F.M. *Manual para Administrar los Santos Sacramentos de Penitencia, Eucharistía, Extremaunción, y Matrimonio, dar Gracias Despues de Comulgar, y Ayudar a Bien Morir, etc.*, Mexico, 1760.

Garrison, George P. *Texas, a Contest of Civilizations*. Boston, 1903.

Hackett, Charles Wilson. *The Revolt of the Pueblo Indians of New Mexico in 1680*, in *Texas State Historical Association Quarterly*, XV, 93–148.

Kenney, M. M. *Tribal Society Among the Texas Indians*, in *Texas State Historical Association Quarterly*, I, 26–34.

Hughes, Anne E. *The Beginnings of Spanish Settlement in the El Paso District*, in *University of California Publications in History*, I, 295–392.

Hodge, Frederick Webb. *Handbook of American Indians North of Mexico*, Bureau of American Ethnology, *Bulletin 30*, Washington, 1907–1910. 2 vols.

Marshall, Thomas Maitland. *A History of the Western Boundary of the Louisiana Purchase, 1819–1841*. Berkeley, 1914.

McCaleb, Walter Flavius. *Some Obscure Points in the Mission Period*, *Texas State Historical Association Quarterly*, I, 216–225.

Fray Geronimo de Mendieta. O.F.M. *Historia Ecclesiastica Indiana*, Joaquin Garcia Icazbalceta Ed., Mexico, 1870.

Sources

Palóu, Fray Francisco, O.F.M. *Relación Historica de la Vida y Apostolicas Tareas del Venerable Padre Fray Junipero Serra.* Mexico, 1787.

Noticias de la Nueva California, Translated and Edited by Herbert E. Bolton. Berkeley, 1926, 4 vols.

Portillo, Esteban L. *Apuntes para la Historia Antigua de Coahuila y Texas.* Saltillo, 1880.

Recopilación de Leyes de los Reynos de las Indias, etc. Tercera Edicion. Madrid, 1774.

Shelby, Charmion Clair. *St. Denis' Second Expedition to the Rio Grande,* in *Southwestern Historical Quarterly,* XXVII, 190-217.

St. Denis' Declaration Concerning Texas in 1717, in *Southwestern Historical Quarterly,* XXVI, 165-183.

West, Elizabeth Howard. *De León's Expedition of 1689,* in *Texas State Historical Association Quarterly,* IX, 199-224.

Bonilla's Brief Compendium of the History of Texas, 1772, in *Texas State Historical Association Quarterly,* VIII, 1-78.

VITA.

Name, Thomas P. O'Rourke, C.S.B., A.M. Born, Lorena, Texas. Date of birth, May 22, 1889. High school, St. Basil's College, Waco, Texas. College, Assumption College, Sandwich, Ontario. Theology, St. Basil's Scholasticate, Toronto, Canada. Ordained, June 29, 1916. Master of Arts, June, 1925, Catholic University of America. Studies at Catholic University: Major, Dr. Guilday; First Minor, Dr. P. J. McCormick; Second Minor, Dr. Leo F. Stock.

INDEX

Abad, Father, 59, 60.
Adaes, 50, 51, 56, 58, 78, 97.
Administration of the Missions, 105-128.
Agreda, María, de Jesús de, 8.
Aguayo, Margués de, 49, 50, 51, 52.
Aguayo, San José de, 22, 52.
Ais Indians, 50, 51, 52, 57.
Alabado, 74, 186.
Alamo, 32.
Alarcon, Government, 32, 33.
Alvarez, Fray Juan, 14.
Andrés Juan, 65, 69.
Angelina Rever, 31.
Anglo-Americans, 50.
Apachería, 68, 74.
Apaches, 15, 39, 42, 63, 65, 68, 72, 75, 83, 167, 169.
Aparicio, Father Francisco, 73.
Apostolic Colleges, Querétaro, 22; Zacatecas, 44; San Fernándo, 64.
Approach of the Missionaries to Texas, 8.
Aranda, Father, 68.
Aranzazu, Nuestra Señora de, 61.
Aristorena, 59, 60.
Arizona, 4.
Arricivita, 23, 34, 41, 42, 44, 74, 98, 163.
Assisi, 1, 10, 61.
Atascostíto, el, 56, 59.
Attacapa, 57, 61.
Ayer, Mrs. Edward E., 8, 98.
Ayeta, Father Franciscoe, 14.
Bahia, 51, 79.
Bancroft, 94.
Baños, Father Joachin de, 65, 69, 74.
Baptism, 74, 85, 90, 92.
Barcía, 94.
Barrio, Gov., 40.
Barrios, Gov., 57, 58, 68, 78, 79.
Bautista, San Juan, 30.
Bazaterra, Orobio, 78.
Benavides, Fray Alonso de (Memorial), 8, 9, 11, 94.

Beltrán, Fray Bernaldino, 6.
Bexar, 50.
Bidai, 61.
Bolton, 5, 16, 17, 23, 30, 36, 38, 50, 53, 57, 60, 63, 65, 73, 75, 78, 81, 83, 95, 97.
Boneoy Morales, 78.
Bonilla, Fray Juan, 14.
Bordoy, Fray, 27.
Bosque, 5, 7, 8, 15, 16.
Brazos, 37, 65.
Brushy Creek, 38.
Buenaventura, Fray Dionysio de la, 5.
Bustillo, 79.
Calahorra, Fray, 59, 60.
California, 63, 72, 73, 76, 77, 85, 89, 93, 94.
Camberos, Fray, 51, 52, 54.
Canada, 77.
Candelaría, 40, 41, 63, 73, 75.
Candlemas, 75.
Canos, 60.
Capistrano, San Juan, 31.
Carancaguases, 55.
Caro, Fray, 57, 59.
Casañas, Fray, 27.
Castellanos, Fray, 30.
Catholic Church in Colonial Days, (Shea), 95.
Chambers County, 56.
Chamuscado, 5.
Chavira, Fray, 56, 57, 60.
Charles V, 3.
Cherokee County, 21, 28, 30.
Christian doctrine, 90.
Christians, 39.
Clement XII, 18.
Coahuila, 23, 29, 33, 39, 47, 79.
Colección de Bulas, 18.
College, Zacatecan, 22, 31, 34, 56, 225; Santa Cruz, 68, 69, 90; San Fernando, 63, 65, 69, 70.
Colleges, Apostolic, 18; Zacatecas, 44, San Franando, 64.
Colorado, 10, 33, 38, 97.
Columbus, 1.

Columbus and His Predecessors, (McCarthy), 7.
Comanches, 49, 65, 70, 71.
Concepción, 38, 83, 84.
Cortés, Hernando, 2.
Cujane Indians, 51, 52, 53.
Crónica Seráfica, 44, 56, 90, 95.
Cuevas, Mariano, S. J., 2.
De Leon, 5, 15, 17, 96.
Del Rio, 58.
Doctrina, 86, 87.
Dolores Los, 50, 51, 52.
Dominicans, 2.
Dunn, Wm. Edward, 16, 17, 28, 97, 99.
Durango, 4.
Edwards County, 74.
Echavaría, Fray, 14, 15.
El Paso, 11, 12, 15.
Engelhardt, 4, 18, 27, 49, 50, 81, 85, 86, 87, 97, 98.
Escovar, Fray, 54.
Espinosa, 30, 31, 33, 46, 47, 90-93-98.
Espíritu Santo, 9, 30, 52, 53, 54, 62, 63.
Estela, Fray, 27.
Extreme Unction, 45.
Felipe, Fray, 66.
Fernandians, 18, 63, 65, 72, 75.
Fitzmorris (Four Decades etc.), 98, 99.
Florida, 94.
Fontcubierta, Fray, 27.
Forbes, 88.
Fort St. Louis, 17, 52, 73.
Fortuni, Fray, 27.
FOUR DECADES OF CATHOLICISM IN TEXAS (Fitzmorris), 76.
Franciscian Missions in Texas, 3, 17, 22, 27, 41, 43, 52, 63, 65, 76, 77, 80, 89, 98.
Franciscans, Coming of, to New Spain, 1-10.
French in Texas, 17, 25, 28, 49, 51, 93, 94.
Galván, 68.
Galve, de, 28.
Ganzábal, Fray, 41, 42, 73.
García of Padilla, Fray, 2.
García, Fray Dugo, 34.
García, Fray, Martin, 37.
García, Fray Pedro, 27.

Garcitas River, 97.
Garsa, Fray, 61.
Garza, Fray, 50, 62, 63.
Gigedo, Revilla, 41, 55.
Goliad, 53, 55, 63.
Gonzales, Fray, 12.
Gregory XVI, 18.
Guadalupe, River, 42.
Guadalajara, 78.
Guadalupe, 44, 49, 52, 61, 62, 67.
Guadalupe, Virgin of, 26.
Guapites, 53, 53, 55.
Guatemala, 45.
Gulf Coast, 29, 33, 38, 60, 77.
Heimbucher, 2.
Hernaez, 18.
Hidalgo, Fray Francisco, 26, 27, 30, 67, 80.
Hierro, Fray Simon, 56.
History, Sources for Texas Catholic, 94-102.
Hodge, F. W., 98.
Holy Cross Mission at Querétaro, 17.
Houston, 21, 61.
Hughes, A. E., (El Paso District), 10, 14.
Hume, W. W., 98.
Hurtado, Fray Nicolas, 14.
Indians, 17, 23, 39, 40, 44, 53, 55, 56, 66, 71, 86, 93.
Indians Lipan, 65.
Indians, Christian, 66.
Indian Trade, 50.
Indies, 18.
Innocent XI, 18.
Jáuregui, Jacinto de Barriosy, 56.
Jesuits in Mexico, 42.
Jesus, Most Holy Name of, 10.
Júarez, 12.
Jumanos, 10, 15, 96.
Junta, Royal, 47.
Karankawan, 40, 51, 53, 53, 62.
King, 66.
Kirwin, (History etc.), 98.
Larios, Fray Juan, 5, 15.
La Salle, 5, 16, 17, 52.
Lavaca Bay, 97.
LeClercq, Fray Maximus, 17.
Leo X, 2.
Library, Texas State, 98.
Library, Congress, 98.
Linares, 4.

104

Lipans, 67, 69, 70, 72, 73, 74.
Little Forks, 59.
List of Missionary Priests, 43.
López, Fray Francisco, 5, 16.
López, Juan Fray, 10, 68.
López, Fray Nicholas, 96.
Louisiana, 49, 58, 97.
Lummis, C. F., 98.
Madrid, 18.
Manuel de la Cruz, Br., 15.
Marcos de Niza, Fray, 4.
Margil, Fray Antonio, 18, 33, 44, 46, 49, 50, 53, 62, 98.
Mariano, Fray, 34, 37, 39, 40, 41, 42, 67.
Martín, Fray, 3.
Martínez, Captain, 25, 26.
Martínez, Fray Alonso, 6.
Martos, Gov., 59.
Massanet, Fray Damian, 5, 15, 17, 27, 29, 96.
Matagorda Bay, 16.
McCarthy, Charles Hallan, (Columbus etc.), 1.
Melchior of Jesus, Fray, 44.
Membré Fray Zenobiuz, 17.
Memorial, (Benavides), 8, 9.
Menard County, 69.
Menardville, 65, 69.
Mendoza, Capt Dominguez, 5, 16.
Mendoza, Expedition, 96.
Mesquía, Fray Perez de, 30.
Mexico, 9, 18, 33, 44, 62, 77, 83, 96.
Mexico City, 18, 27, 28, 45, 52.
Molina, Fray Miguel 70.
Milam County, 34.
Miranda, Antonio, 27.
Miranda, Bernardo de, 68.
Missions, administration, 105-128.
Missions—chronological list, 22; names of Texas, 21; Espíritu Santo, de Zuniga, 22, 52, Purisima Concepcion, 29, Nuestra Señora de la Luz, 56; de la Candelaria, 22, 75, del Rosário, 52; de Refugio, 61, Guadalupe, 46; San Francisco de los Texas, 23; Santísimo Nombre de María, 27; de los Neches, 29; San Antonio de Valero, 22, 31; San José, 29, San Xavier, 22, 38; San Ildefonso, 39; San Miguel, 22, 51; Santa Cruz, 72, San Lorenzo, 72, San Sabá, 65; San José de los Nazones, 22; San Francisco de le Espada, 22, San Juan Capistrano, 22; San Marcos, 22.
Mississippi, 17, 29, 77.
Molina, Fray, 37, 61.
Morfi, 95.
Mound Prairie, 30.
Munoz, Fray Pedro, 32.
Nacogdoches, 46, 49, 50, 51, 59, 62, 98.
Natchitoches, 96, 97.
Navarrete, 59.
Navarro, Fray Sebastian, 14.
Naxera, Fray Manuel de, 33.
Nazones, 30.
Neches Indians, 38, 30.
Neches River, 23, 32, 61.
New Braunfels, 42.
New Spain, 94.
New Mexico, 4, 9, 28, 81.
Nueces, 63, 75.
Nuestra Señora de Guadalupe College, 18.
Nuestra Señora de Guadalupe, 46, 49.
Nuestra Señora de los Dolores, 38, 50.
Nuestra Señora de la Luz, 57.
Nuestra Señora del Refugio, 63.
O'Callaghan, 94.
Olivares, Fray, 31, 32.
Oñate Juan de, 6, 8.
Orcoquisac El, 56, 59, 61.
Orcoquiza, 57, 59, 60.
Ortiz, Fray, 38, 42, 73.
O'Shea, J. F., 95.
Our Lady of Guadalupe, 53, 63, 69.
Our Lady of La Candelaria, 63.
Our Lady of Light, 56, 58, 59, 60, 61.
Our Lady of Rosary Mission, 53, 63.
Our Lady of Refuge, 61, 63.
Our Lady of Sorrows, 53, 58, 63, 70.
Pacheco, Don Rafael Martínez, 57, 59, 60.
Pajalat, 38.
Palóu, 71, 73, 73, 94.
Parédes, Fray Miguel de, 31.
Parras, 18.

Parrilla, Captain Diego, 65, 69, 72.
Paso de la Cruz, 68.
Payays, 32.
Pecos, 16.
Penasco, Fray Juan Dionysio, 15.
Pensacola, 16.
Pérez, Fray Juan, 1.
Perras, Fray Pedro, 73.
Peru, 83.
Pilar de Bucareli, 49, 62.
Piszina, Manuel Ramirez, 53.
Proto-Martyrs, 4.
Province of Holy Gospel, 4.
Pueblos, 88.
Querétaro, College of, 3, 4, 17, 18, 26, 34, 42, 44, 65, 68, 73, 89, 95.
Querétaran Missions, 18, 23, 33, 36, 39, 42, 49, 65, 73.
Quivira, 9, 16.
Rábago, 40, 42, 68, 73, 74.
Raines, (Bibliography of Texas), 99.
Ramon, Diego, 42.
Real County, 74.
Refugio, 76.
Rio de las Nueces, 11.
Rio Frio, 31.
Rio Guadalupe, 31.
Rio Grande, 16, 17, 33, 37, 38, 47, 56, 65, 69, 74.
Rio de las Nueces, 73.
Rio San Antonio, 31.
Rivera, Pedra de, 31.
Rockdale, 97.
Rodríguez, Fray Agustín, 5.
Romero, Fray, 59.
Rosary Mission, 52, 54, 55, 62.
Rubí Marqués de, 57, 73.
Sabine, 30.
Sacrosancti Apostolatus, 18.
Salas Juthe Juan de, 10.
Salazar, Fray Cristóbal, 7, 14.
Saltillo, 69, 78.
San Antonio de Valero, 33, 37, 38, 41, 52, 56, 62, 65, 67, 76, 77, 84, 97.
San Augustine, 50, 52, 53, 63.
San Bernardo, 37.
San Buenaventura, Fray Juan, 15.
Sánchez, Fray Benito, 30.
Sandoval, 78.
San Fernándo, 4, 18, 75, 76, 95.
San Francisco Mission, 34, 37, 61, 83, 99.
San Gabriel River, 34, 36, 65, 73.
Santa Gertrudis, 63.
San Ildefonso, 40.
San Jacinto, 61.
San Juan, 34, 51, 69, 83.
San Lorenzo, 74.
San Marcos, 42.
San Pedro Creek, 23.
San Sabá Mission, 42, 65, 66, 68, 73, 97.
Santa Ana, Fray Benito de, 32, 37, 38, 40, 68, 69.
Santa Cruz de San Salba, 63, 73.
Santa María, Fray Agustín, 5, 14.
Santa Hermandad, 79.
Santa Rosa, Arroyo de, 61.
Santiago, 72.
Santiesteban, Fray, 69, 70, 72, 74.
Santísimo Nombre de María, 21, 28.
San Xavier, 38, 39, 41, 42, 69.
Satereyn, Fray Marcos, 57.
Serra, Junipero, 63, 71, 72, 73, 76, 89.
Shea, John Gilmary, 44, 94, 95.
Silva, 67.
Soledad, La, 12.
Solis, Fray Gaspar José de, 29.
Sonora, 4.
Sources for Texas Catholic History, 94-102.
Spanish Cortes, 76.
Spanish Franciscans, 52.
Sparks, Jared, 94.
Spring Creek, 61.
Tamiques, 53.
Tiguayo, 16.
Terán, Don Domingo de los Riós, 27, 28, 32.
Tertiaries, 27.
Terreros, Fray Alsonso Giroldo de, 41, 65, 71, 72, 73.
Terreros, Don Pedro, 68, 73, 75, 83.
Texas, 8, 10, 11, 15, 21, 31, 40, 44, 28, 69, 72, 76, 77, 89, 95.
Texas Indians, 16, 27, 30, 47.
Tiguas, 19.
Tlascaltecans, 61, 69.
Toribio, 67.
Torquemada, 94.
Trinity River, 47, 56, 58, 60.
Truxillo, Fray José de, 14.

"Twelve Apostles", 3.
Urbano, Collegio (Rome), 22.
Valdez, Fray Jose, 14.
Valencia, 44.
Valero, San Antonio de, 52.
Valero, Viceroy, 31, 34, 47, 51.
Vallejo, Fray, 51, 52, 53, 59.
Valasco, Fray Mariano, 63.
Vera Cruz, 44.
Vergara, Fray Gabriel, 30.
Victoria, 52.
Winthuisen, 78.
Xarame Indians, 31, 52, 53.
Xavier River, 39.
Ximénez, Fray Diego, 65, 69, 73, 74.
Yucatan, 44.
Ybarbo, Gil, 50.
Zacatecas, 42, 43, 44, 85, 89, 95.
Zacatecas College, 43.
Zacatecan Missions, 18, 30, 33, 40, 44, 46, 49, 50, 53, 59, 62, 67, 69.
Zavaleta Fray, 16.
Zevallos, 65.
Zumárraga, Juan de, 3.